CONSTRUCTING A BETTER TOMORROW

A Logical Look to Reform America

NICHOLAS BEARNS

CONSTRUCTING A BETTER TOMORROW
A LOGICAL LOOK TO REFORM AMERICA

iUniverse books may be ordered through booksellers or by contacting:

iUniverse
1663 Liberty Drive
Bloomington, IN 47403
www.iuniverse.com
1-800-Authors (1-800-288-4677)

Because of the dynamic nature of the Internet, any web addresses or links contained in this book may have changed since publication and may no longer be valid. The views expressed in this work are solely those of the author and do not necessarily reflect the views of the publisher, and the publisher hereby disclaims any responsibility for them.

Any people depicted in stock imagery provided by Thinkstock are models, and such images are being used for illustrative purposes only. Certain stock imagery © Thinkstock.

ISBN: 978-1-5320-0629-6 (sc)
ISBN: 978-1-5320-0630-2 (e)

Library of Congress Control Number: 2016914206

Print information available on the last page.

iUniverse rev. date: 08/27/2016

Contents

My Goal

Over the last several decades, the stories of our great nation are beginning to be replaced. They are being replaced by the reality of diminished opportunity, a crumbling infrastructure, and a failed federal government. From unjust wars fought in the Middle East to Washington giving billions of dollars to wealthy individuals and corporations. All this waste of life, money, and resources while many Americans are unemployed, homeless, and starving. Some, working sixty or more hours at several jobs to keep food on the table for them and their families.

I was very fortunate that this was not the kind of America I grew up in. Many others are not that fortunate, and what bothers me most is that our nation does not allow for all its citizens to succeed. If we truly are the greatest and wealthiest nation in the world, then why does our nation still face inhumane problems? A great nation wherein there remains homelessness, starvation, and unemployment is not a great nation.

Originally, each generation left a better world for their kids to inherit and continue to build upon. Current federal policies have crippled the *American Dream*, and the opposite is now in effect. As we continue to allow politicians to do the bidding of large corporations, the well-being of working class Americans continues to decline. With only the needs of private interests being addressed by politicians at all levels of government, we have seen a dramatic decline in the living standards of the average American.

Our nation is not beyond saving, but a nation is only as strong as its weakest citizen. With our current system, the government has stolen our rights as citizens to succeed, and have broken the social contract. The governed will cease allowing consent to this government while it continues to ignore the interests of all Americans. For these reasons, I will try to offer a plausible solution to undo the damage caused by crony capitalism, and corrupt politicians.

Several departments in the federal government and how certain programs function must be redesigned for the **21**st century. By ignoring issues for decades from a gridlocked Congress, our whole nation is near disaster. We have an overly complicated tax system that does not provide enough tax revenue to balance the federal budget. A budget that includes billions of dollars in wasteful spending, all while ignoring the needs of every American.

The ideas I am about to propose are neither to be considered right or wrong. This is a solution I crafted by revision of how taxes shall be collected, and more importantly how those dollars will be spent. With a corrupt campaign finance system, politicians have failed us by not creating legislation to better our nation. In order to implement a change that removes corruption form the system, and protects the welfare of all US citizens can only be done by the creation of a new constitutional amendment.

As things stand right now, not many politicians care about those who elect them. They don't have to because the legality of super PACs funded by the millionaires and billionaires, are the ones they work for. On the bright side, you can at least note that there is one thing that can bring bipartisanship to Congress. Both parties, Democrats & Republicans alike, love this system. Through a system of basically legal bribery, allows for people of wealth and influence to control what legislation passes or does not pass through Congress, so that it may benefit them.

There is no one simple answer to fix our entire political system. Due to the inaction of a majority of politicians, it is why I have put research into how every program currently functions. By understanding how all tax revenue is collected, and how those taxes are spent, we can understand how it can be changed to benefit all involved. In order to create change in our many government programs, the same process had to be applied.

If the amendment I propose is passed as is, that would be fantastic. However, that is not my primary purpose in doing this. Despite massive corruption in our political system, there are some politicians that have remained focus on implementing policy to improve our nation. It is policies such as raising the minimum wage, creating a single-payer healthcare system, and fixing our corrupt election and campaign finance systems that I believe will restore the American dream. While there may be many solutions to create these programs, the following chapters discuss how the current system works, and how they can be improved.

Everything written and included in this book is for the sole purpose of informing our populace. Despite the many arguments for raising the minimum wage, and creating better welfare programs, our many politicians still refuse to act. Only once all Americans understand how programs like a single-payer health insurance system is superior to our current mess; can we as a country unite and demand the change desperately needed.

Whether the next amendment to our constitution is the same or completely different from what I propose, it is important that we begin the conversation about what solutions to our country's problems could look like. That is the goal of this book. Time is running out for our nation, as a complex government system is causing strain on citizens, businesses, and even the government programs themselves. If we do not solve these problems, and continue to allow our democracy to be repressed by the current oligarchy in power, we will no longer remain the United States of America.

The Tax System

The federal tax structure has not had major structural changes since President Reagan in **1986**. Thirty years later, businesses face the highest taxes in the world. Employees while typically receiving tax refunds at the end of the year, often do not make enough to remain financially stable. Meanwhile, those at the top of the brackets. The millionaires and billionaires of companies are reporting record profits and record incomes.

Currently the system is not that of what Regan had envisioned when signing that bill into law. Reagan's economic policies were inspired by the *Trickle-Down Theory*. This idea stating that with lower tax rates and burdens on businesses, they can then afford to pay their employees more, and invest more in their businesses. Unfortunately, Reagan was only half right.

While it is true with less taxes, businesses will have more money. The sad reality is that they will only pay their workers as much as they legally have to. Until we raise the minimum wage, businesses will only continue to pay the minimum. It is time to change the tax system one last time to benefit us all, and not just the few.

A Balanced Budget

Before proposing changes to the tax system and how funds are spent, we must first look at how it is done currently. By understanding the current flaws in the present structure, a better proposal can be created to solve all current problems our nation is facing.

Currently there is very little transparency in government. With the tax code being at **74,608** pages long as reported by the *Washington Examiner*, it is no wonder why everyone is confused. For any government to operate, it must not only be able to have a strong economic system, but also must have a fair taxation system so the government can function, thus allowing businesses and individuals to succeed.

As things are now, businesses are facing the highest taxes in the world with an on average **35%** tax rate and only goes higher once state and local taxes are calculated. These high taxes have caused two problems, the first being companies have relocated their offices oversees to avoid these taxes. The result leading to many jobs being moved oversees as well. Secondly, for the companies that remain, a large portion of revenue is devoted to paying these taxes, and for an army of accountants to understand the current system.

With the current system as complex as it is, the only way forward is to reduce the burden created by these complexities. What can be created is a causation of success if the government can operate effectively again. And in doing so government must begin to govern businesses and not businesses governing the government.

Before we can propose a fix to this mess, we must first look at how much money the federal government is spending annually. Once all expenditures are listed, it can be determined which ones are necessary to keep, which can be eliminated, and which programs need to be reformed. By finding the approximate costs for all programs, we can then revise the system in which tax revenue is collected. When making changes to this system, we can create a framework that can finally guarantee a balanced budget.

The next image shows how all collected revenue was spent from the years of **2012 – 2015.** At the bottom also shows the deficit amounts and total federal debt for each of those years.

Spending by the US Government 2012 – 2015

Spending Category	2012	2013	2014	2015
Pensions	819.5 Billion	870.9 Billion	914.6 Billion	953.6 Billion
Health Care	818.5 Billion	856.1 Billion	921.1 Billion	1.028 Trillion
Education	103.3 Billion	85.3 Billion	102.6 Billion	133.8 Billion
Defense	849.6 Billion	818.6 Billion	799.8 Billion	797.9 Billion
Welfare	411.2 Billion	397.8 Billion	370.3 Billion	361.9 Billion
Protection	35.7 Billion	34.1 Billion	32.9 Billion	34.0 Billion
Transportation	93.0 Billion	91.7 Billion	91.9 Billion	89.5 Billion
General Governemnt	50.6 Billion	49.0 Billion	44.4 Billion	43.7 Billion
Other Spending	135.1 Billion	30.3 Billion	0.4 Billion	22.4 Billion
Interest	220.4 Billion	220.9 Billion	229.0 Billion	223.2 Billion
Total Spending	3.537 Trillion	3.454 Trillion	3.506 Trillion	3.688 Trillion
Federal Defecit	1.087 Trillion	679.6 Billion	484.6 Billion	438.4 Billion
Total US Debt	16.050 Trillion	16.719 Trillion	17.794 Trillion	18.120 Trillion

Data From: http://www.usfederalbudget.us/federal_budget_detail_2015bs22015n#usgs302

The national debt is now over **19** trillion dollars as of **2016**. The decades of reckless spending and foreign wars has left us with a huge financial strain. The interest payment on the debt alone was **$223.2** billion in **2015**, which shamefully, is almost double the amount spent on education that same year. It should be expected that our tax dollars are being spent properly. In reality, areas like education and infrastructure have been criminally underfunded. The results being an infrastructure crumbling without enough educated people to fix it.

Additionally, **$1.028** trillion was spent on *Health Care* in fiscal **2015**. This is approximately equal to the *Department of Health and Human Services'* budget that year according to their website. The total costs of Medicaid and Medicare totaled to **85%** of that budget. With the introduction of the *Affordable Care Act* (ACA) it did increase the number of those insured in our nation, but has still failed to provide a fair healthcare system and insure everyone. Despite **28%** of the federal budget being devoted to healthcare, there are few who benefit.

If citizens pay their taxes, then it is only fair for all citizens to benefit from government services. One common argument used by those against any use of federal funds for social programs will state it is not the government's job. That the government is not responsible for the well-being of every citizen on its soil. The problem with that line-of-thought is that our constitution already delegates this task to the United States Congress. As stated in *Article I, Section 8:*

The Congress shall have Power To lay and collect Taxes, Duties, Imposts and Excises, to pay the Debts and provide for the common Defence and general Welfare of the United States; but all Duties, Imposts and Excises shall be uniform throughout the United States…

Even the founders believed that any money taken in by congressional authority, should then be used to either pay debts, pay for our military, or be used for the welfare of our people. It is a disgrace to be the wealthiest country in the world with a populace starving, homeless or uneducated. In many cases, the millions of Americans living in poverty result in a combination of those problems.

It is time to allow all Americans to realize their full potential. To move forward, we need to rethink a majority of federal procedures and programs. Starting with the tax system, we need to plan how much money, and how it is raised. The next step is creating a budget to allocate the tax revenue so that it goes to programs which benefits all citizens. One of the many reasons tax proposals fail is because they try to solve every problem based on how much money they take in, and reduce programs if necessary to balance the budget. The problem with this is that there are fundamental areas of government in which money needs to be apportioned to and thus must be continually funded.

A frustration I have with Congress is every year hearing them bicker about how funds should be spent. Now this is a topic that does have to be discussed yearly, as in any business or household. The frustration comes from the fact that several congress members would rather see the government shutdown rather than pass a budget. The reasons why vary, but the reasons never justify a shutdown of the federal government. The results of a shutdown mean educational and health programs cease operation, and those on welfare would no longer receive their financial assistance. This should not and can no longer be an option for those in Congress to have as some sort of leverage over some ideological issue.

For a fair taxation system that funds the government and benefits the welfare of all Americans, a new framework must be created under a new constitutional amendment. Although it states how funds can be collected, it does not state how they should be spent. After Franklin D. Roosevelt passed the *New Deal* legislation during his administration from **1933** to **1945**, he laid the groundwork for how the government can truly provide for the general welfare of the United States.

My proposal is that Congress must make budgets based on percentage distribution of federal funds to government departments, and specific purposes. Instead of

Congress debating on how many billions of dollars go to programs and areas of government, they debate on a percentage of total revenue to be distributed to federal departments and specific purposes.

It is the responsibility of those departments to appropriately budget these funds and inform Congress of additional funds when necessary. For example, instead of how we currently estimate of much money we will need to pay out for Social Security, Medicare and Medicaid, education etc. the debate would be about what percentage of tax revenue would be enough to fund these departments. The next page shows a chart depicting the spending in **2015** broken down by percentage.

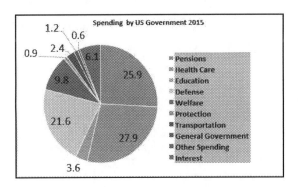

The biggest change for this to work requires taxes to no longer being raised for specific purposes. Rather all taxes shall be collected by the IRS, then the collected revenue will be distributed to each department dependent on the percentage agreed to by Congress. With a system like this, taxes can be created that will increase tax revenue naturally with population and economic increases.

For example, social security benefits and healthcare costs will never be a fixed cost. As the population grows, those requiring these services will increase as well. In order for these programs to maintain funding properly, revenue collected through taxes needs to be able to adjust quickly to the needs of these programs. It would also be necessary for those who oversee the costs of healthcare and social security to report to Congress and state weather or not they are have enough funds for projected costs.

In this system it will also allow surpluses to remain in their accounts to accommodate for any unexpected costs such as epidemics and natural disasters. One important fact to remember is that the costs of social security will continue to grow as more people live longer lives as others qualify daily for the program. Thus any money apportioned to this purpose should be able to increase easily with it. Thus if enough money is coming in to fund our current programs, then if the population grows, even though more money will be needed to pay out for those programs, the larger population will be able to sustain the difference without major changes to the system.

So before we discuss how the money should be spent, lets first look at a system then can raise enough money for the government to operate. Once we have a system in place that can provide the basics, we can then discuss the unseen potential of our nation.

Current Revenue

The sixteenth amendment of the US Constitution which was submitted for ratification **July 12, 1909** and ratified on **February 3, 1913** reads:

> *The Congress shall have power to lay and collect taxes on incomes, from whatever source derived, without apportionment among the several States, and without regard to any census or enumeration.*

This is the amendment giving Congress the authority to tax our incomes. Over the years since, how these taxes on both people and businesses have changed many times. For how individuals are taxed, the most recent structure is shown below:

Image From: *http://www.bankrate.com/finance/taxes/tax-brackets.aspx*

2015 tax brackets (for taxes due April 18, 2016)				
Tax rate	Single filers	Married filing jointly or qualifying widow/widower	Married filing separately	Head of household
10%	Up to $9,225	Up to $18,450	Up to $9,225	Up to $13,150
15%	$9,226 to $37,450	$18,451 to $74,900	$9,226 to $37,450	$13,151 to $50,200
25%	$37,451 to $90,750	$74,901 to $151,200	$37,451 to $75,600	$50,201 to $129,600
28%	$90,751 to $189,300	$151,201 to $230,450	$75,601 to $115,225	$129,601 to $209,850
33%	$189,301 to $411,500	$230,451 to $411,500	$115,226 to $205,750	$209,851 to $411,500
35%	$411,501 to $413,200	$411,501 to $464,850	$205,751 to $232,425	$411,501 to $439,000
39.6%	$413,201 or more	$464,851 or more	$232,426 or more	$439,001 or more

As shown there are seven rates in which people can fall under based on income, and four filing categories resulting in twenty-eight brackets different brackets that your return can be filed under. More importantly is the fact the IRS then has to validate not only numerical discrepancies in these returns, but are also checking if you filed in the correct bracket.

This alone would be a burden, but I haven't even mentioned all the possible tax credits that can be redeemed, and all the possible ways for fraud and mistakes to occur. Nevertheless, this is the current system so let's estimate to see how much revenue is generated from this complex system.

The next chart attempts to estimate how much revenue the income tax generates. Using data from an article on taxfoundation.org published **October 15ᵗʰ 2015**, I used their figures from the IRS of tax year **2013**. This data is the amount of households that paid taxes in each bracket. Using those figures and the minimum amount of yearly income reported to in each bracket I multiplied them together to approximate how much revenue each bracket is generating to find a total. When I discuss the new tax brackets and estimate that amount, I will be using the same framework.

An important note to consider with this framework, I am not calculating in the average deductions and credits that our system currently has. For example, those in the **15%** bracket on average paid only **6.5%** in taxes. To keep it simple I am keeping the percentages as they are written. Based on that I believe my estimate then should be close to or maybe a little higher than the actual amount collected in **2013**.

	Bankrate.com	Tax Foundation.org	(Taxpayers)*(Minimum Filer Amt.)*(% Rate)
Tax Rates	Single filers	Taxpayers	Estimate Income Tax Rev.
0%		36,860,716	$0.00
10%	< $9,225	27,400,094	$25,276,586,720
15%	$9,226 - $37,450	42,195,123	$58,393,830,720
25%	$37,451 - $90,750	24,009,141	$224,791,584,900
28%	$90,751 - $189,300	4,603,602	$116,978,815,800
33%	$189,301 - $411,500	1,768,562	$110,480,883,200
35%	$411,501 - 413,200	176,838	$25,469,154,840
39.6%	> $413,201	892,420	$146,024,539,200
	Totals:	137,906,496	$707,415,395,380

Now the first item that should cause you to question right away, is the **38.6** million households that paid zero in income taxes. As stated by taxfoundation.org, *"This occurs when a household's income is less than the value of the deductions and personal exemptions it is able to claim. (Greenberg)"* Why this annoys me the most is that if you have an income, then you should be paying your fair percentage of taxes as well. I do understand that these households are making less than **$9,225** a year. However, anyone who earns an income should be paying their fair share which at minimum is currently **10%**.

This is also why a minimum wage of **$15.00** an hour needs to be implemented. It is an embarrassment to think that you can earn an income through either a full or part time position, but still need government assistance to maintain stability. The whole point of a job is to maintain stability in life.

Most Americans know, living paycheck to paycheck and relying on government assistance is not a stable life. If we are the richest country in the world, surely there is enough wealth for all of us to prosper, and enough jobs for the American people to earn their living. For the continued welfare of this nation, it is thus the federal government's responsibility to make sure that its populace maintains employment.

How the government can go about doing this I will discuss in more detail in a later chapter. What is important about the ideology is that the more people you have employed making a living wage, the revenue generated through the income tax grows. For this reason, the incentive for job growth becomes a greater priority for the federal government. Our national and state policies can start to focus more on promoting and investing in new industries and scientific advancements once we pay for the basic necessities again in a competent way.

So for the **137.9** million households that filed taxes, my estimate using the lowest income earned in each bracket was **$707.4** billion. Now understanding the variances that were not calculated in my estimate, the actual amount collected by the IRS in **2013** was about **1.316** trillion dollars. A difference of about **$600** billion from my calculated method. In two ways this surprises me in positive ways. The first being despite the complexity of the system, and huge potential for fraud and or error, the IRS were still able to collect this much. The second being I had originally thought that the combinations of tax deductions, and credits would have caused taxes to decrease significantly more.

Revenue Source	2013	
Individual Income Tax	1.316	Trillion
Corporate Income Tax	273.5	Billion
Social Insurance Taxes	947.8	Billion
Excise Taxes	83.0	Billion
Other	153.4	Billion
Total Revenue	2.775	Trillion

Data From: *http://www.usgovernmentrevenue.com/*
year_revenue_2013USbn_17bs1n#usgs302

In the same year **2.775** trillion dollars were collected in total by all revenue sources. The derived sources are broken down in the chart above. The *Individual Income Tax* we have previously discussed. The *Corporate Income Tax* gets trickier to explain given the many regulations and credits regarding businesses. This is one of the reasons why in my proposal, there is no federal corporate income tax. In return for no federal tax they will pay their employees a living wage of **$15.00** an hour minimum.

The *Social Insurance Taxes* include the revenue generated from the *Federal Insurance Contributions Act* (FICA). This includes the additional **6.2%** taxed on income as noted by *Social Security* on paystubs, and **1.45%** noted by *Medicare*. This is a common truth most Americans don't know, that their pay is being taxed an additional **7.45%** every pay period on top of what they pay depending on their tax bracket. So realistically if your income places you in the **10%** bracket, the lowest bracket, your take home pay is reduced **17.45%** from federal taxes alone before state and local taxes get calculated.

Now of course at the end of the year, the current system allows for many deductions and credits for taxpayers. According to some estimates, as high as eight out of ten taxpayers will receive a tax refund. Problem being is obtaining a tax refund does not help financial stability throughout the rest of the year. At the current minimum hourly rate, an employee will take home **$580** gross pay every two weeks, as most companies have bi-weekly payrolls. After the federal taxes alone they will have **$478.79**. For someone living on their own with minimal expenses and living in one of the seven states that has no income tax, then maybe with a cheap apartment to rent, a budget can be made.

This is just not the case anymore though. People need to earn more to maintain a stable life. In my area of Pennsylvania for example, many apartment complexes will not allow you to rent there unless your monthly income is approximately three times the rent. So for a one-bedroom apartment at around **$850** a month, the average price for a suburban area apartment, you have to earn **$2550** each month. Broken down to an hourly wage, you would have to earn **$15.94**. Now this is for someone who is trying to rent a one-bedroom. This is outrageous. Someone who earns enough money to pay the rent costs should be able to rent it.

Of course there are other apartment complexes that may be cheaper, and those owners have every right to charge their rentals as they see fit. However, it does add to the argument why the minimum wage needs to be raised.

Excise taxes is the other main area of focus to raise revenue. These taxes are commonly placed on products in which the consumer pays at time of purchase. We currently have an excise tax on alcohol and tobacco which in **2013** accounted for **$24.4** billion. We also have excise taxes on gasoline dealing with highway and airport transportation. I am not sure under which legislation this is from, but accounted for **$49.4** billion in revenue. In total all excise taxes raised **$83** billion.

I believe these to be currently underused by Congress to generate revenue. There are some in place on certain tobacco products, wines, beers, gas, and a few others. The following is the most recent list of federal excise taxes I could find and their respective rates.

Federal Excise Tax Rates for 2008
Data From: http://taxfoundation.org/article/federal-excise-tax-rates-1944-2008-selected-years

Liquor taxes:

Distilled spirits (per proof gallon)	$13.50
Still wines (per wine gallon):	
Not over 14% alcohol	$1.07
Over 14 to 21% alcohol	$1.57
Over 21 to 24% alcohol	$3.15
Beer (per 31-gallon barrel)	$18

Tobacco taxes:

Small cigars, not over 3 lbs. per thousand	$1.828
Large cigars, over 3 lbs. per thousand	$48.75
Cigarettes (per thousand, 3 lbs. or less)	$19.50–$40.95
Pipe tobacco (per pound)	$1.10

Manufacturers' excise taxes:

Gasoline (per gallon)	18.4¢
Highway tires (per pound respectively)	(f)
Trucks (sale price)	12%
Firearms, shells, cartridges (sale price)	11%
Pistols and revolvers (sale price)	10%
Bows (sale price)	11%
Arrow shafts	42¢
Fishing equipment (sale price)	10%
Gas guzzler tax (for fuel inefficient cars)	1,000 to $7,700

Miscellaneous excise taxes:

Local telephone service (amount paid)	3%
Toll/Long distance telephone service (amount paid)	—
Transportation of persons by air (amount paid)	(d)

International departure ticket	$15.10 (e)
Air freight (domestic waybills)	6.25%
Wagers (amount wagered except parimutuel)	0.25%
Occupation of accepting wagers (per year)	$50

Foreign insurance policies (premium paid):

Life insurance	—
Other insurance	—

Coal sales, underground and surface mines (per ton, respectively)	$1.10, 55¢

Environmental ("superfund") excise taxes:

Crude oil (per barrel)	5¢
Chemicals (per ton)	Varies

Retailers' excise taxes:

Jewelry (sale price)	—
Furs (sale price)	—
Diesel fuel for highway vehicles (per gallon)	24.4¢
Gasoline substitute fuels for highway vehicles and motor boats	—
Gasoline used in noncommercial aviation (per gallon)	19.4¢
Noncommercial aviation fuel other than gasoline (per gallon)	21.9¢
Inland waterways users' fuel (per gallon)	20.1¢
Gasohol (per gallon)	12.35¢ to 13.25¢

Unfortunately, **2008** is the most recent data of all excise taxes I could find. I am not entirely sure how these have all changed with this being eight years out of date. Regardless, the same problem exists in this system. As stated earlier, Congress does have the power to raise excises; however, they are all to be uniform. It can be argued the current system is uniform in that depending on the product, that rate is used across the US.

My problem with this system, is once again a recurring problem I observe in the federal government. That is another system too complicated to truly be beneficial.

While some products are taxed at a percentage base, which I believe all excises should be, there are many taxed by dollar amounts or some tertiary method. For the products being taxed by dollar amounts such as cigarettes, I do not feel this to be uniform. If one pack of cigarettes cost five dollars and another pack seven dollars, it would make sense for the product with the higher price to also have a higher tax collected from it. With excises based on percentages this is accomplished, and can then be applied to more products in the same category as well.

New Tax Brackets & Excise Taxes

With a system so complicated to understand and even more difficult to enforce, it is time to start discussing a new taxation system. Only a system that is simple and transparent will allow the IRS to properly function. Many tax plans have been released including several in the **2016** presidential primary. Those released range from flat tax plans to more progressive taxes. It would appear though the math is often never really thought through. Experts ranging from economists to financial advisors study the effects of these plans. Commonly the conclusion to many include the deficit growing larger, and often those in the top brackets pay less in taxes.

There is no reason why someone who makes six figures or greater in yearly income should be paying a smaller percentage of taxes than anyone making less. We can simplify the tax system, but all aspects of the revenue generated must be looked at. A reason why many tax plans fail to gain public approval is often they only aim to try and fix the tax brackets and tax credit areas of our system. As discussed earlier, income generated from income taxes alone was **$1.316** trillion in **2013** when total spending was **$3.454** trillion.

So of course, any fix to our tax bracket system and credits therein, will not bring in enough revenue to fund the entire federal government. Although that doesn't stop Republicans and even a few Democrats stating to cut federal programs to decrease spending. Obviously I am not saying our system cannot be fixed, but to fix it, all areas of the federal government where revenue can be earned must be taken into account to make a plan to move forward.

The first problem is the income tax brackets. What bothered me the most is to be in the lower tax bracket for our current system, you had to make less than **$9,225**. Anything above that you were in a higher tax bracket. Yet, the most troubling fact is the one that is not discussed or reported commonly, if ever. That is the federal government does have a minimum wage that is currently set to **$7.25** an hour. For someone working a full time job at that hourly rate for forty hours a week for fifty-two weeks, then they are making **$15,080** gross pay meaning before any federal, state, and local taxes are taken out.

So then why is the bottom tax bracket set to **$9,225** and not **$15,080**. The minimum wage is meant to be a living wage in that any individual that works full time should be able to survive. That is not only my belief, but a belief held by many Americans. Now for someone to make **$9,225** whom is working a full time job as described before, is approximately earning **$4.43** an hour. That is ridiculous and what should be against the law.

In looking at new tax brackets, we can also address the fact that the minimum wage is too low. Later I will discuss why we need the minimum wage raised to **$15.00** an hour, and more importantly how businesses of all sizes can survive this change. For now, let's assume we have this minimum wage. That means anyone working forty hours a week for fifty-two weeks now makes **$31,200** a year before any taxes. This should now be where the bottom bracket is now set to. Below is what a potential bracket system could look like moving forward.

Percentages	Total Income	Take Home Pay (Min)	Income Taxed (Min)
20%	≤ $31,199.99	$24,960	$6,240
25%	$31,200.00 - $99,999.99	$23,400	$7,800
30%	$100,000.00 - $499,999.99	$70,000	$30,000
35%	$500,000.00 - $999,999.99	$325,000	$175,000
50%	≥ 1,000,000.00	$500,000	$500,000

So for anyone who works part time, which would be then the only reason why your making less than the minimum yearly rate, your overall taxes would be **20%** of that income. There are few things to note with this system. The first being that all taxes will be filed individually. This will keep things simple for the IRS to verify all income earned by every individual. Secondly, there will no longer be any tax credits or deductions. The money you earn will be taxed at its proper percent, and that will be the end of it. At the end of each fiscal year like in our current system, all taxable income will be calculated. All taxable income sources include employment, interest on bonds and bank accounts, and from dividends. Income earned through stock investments called *capital gains*, will no longer be considered taxable income. Instead a **5%** excise tax shall be levied against the cost of all trades in US stock markets. This will be discussed more with the excise taxes.

If your total income is in the same bracket as it was taxed throughout the year, then you will neither owe or receive a refund. For a majority of Americans, those earning **$31,200 - $99,999.99** then your taxes will have been deducted correctly assuming all earned income was taxed at **25%**. For those who earn less than **$31,200** they will have a tax refund. This is because a **25%** tax rate would be applied as a minimum for working at **$15.00** an hour. At the end of the year though since their total income was less than that figure, their total income for that year will be retaxed at **20%**.

At the end of the fiscal year, if your total income is in a greater tax bracket than what portions of income were taxed at earlier will cause you to owe. For example, if Goldman Sachs pays a guest speaker **$225,000** for their time giving a speech, the person earning this money will have this income taxed at **30%.** Now for argument if this person did three of these speeches in one year, then they earned **$675,000** minimum. Thus their total income will be retaxed at **35%** assuming they still made less than a million dollars, and will have to pay the difference.

The reason I chose to start the brackets at **20%** is because as stated before, the lowest bracket is already at **17.45%** combining income taxes and FICA taxes. The new system also does away with FICA. The IRS would no longer have to verify which money is coming in from specific taxes, and then redistribute the money to the proper programs. As described earlier, all income collected will be redistributed based on a percentage set by the congressional budget.

While simplifying the government's side of this, it also simplifies the accountant's job for payroll. Now only one federal deduction will occur on any employee's paystub, with its percentage based on how much that paystub is for. It is true that by definition, this would be a tax increase on all American incomes. However, in conjunction with raising the minimum wage, even those receiving the minimum will be earning more after taxes than they are currently.

We also have not yet discussed how the majority of these tax dollars will be used to fund better programs. By raising the minimum wage and increasing job growth, the federal government will only need to finance three social programs. A *Single-Payer Health Insurance Program, Social Security,* and *Disability.* Once we have programs that benefit all Americans, the results will increase the quality of life for all, and justify the new tax system.

So under a system like this, how much income can be generated? In order to answer this, most of the data are estimates based on the data from **2013** and current data. Since several tax brackets are now combined this will cause variance in the estimates along with accounting for everyone making **$15.00** an hour. The IRS had a little over **150** million returns filed for **2015**, so that is the total number of returns I'm using to estimate the new revenue.

Percentages	Total Income	Taxpayers	Estimate Income Tax Rev.
20%	≤ $31,199.99	10,000,000	$62,399,980,000
25%	FTE - $99,999.99	130,000,000	$1,014,000,000,000
30%	$100,000.00 - $499,999.99	8,827,000	$264,810,000,000
35%	$500,000.00 - $999,999.99	1,000,000	$17,500,000,000
50%	≥ 1,000,000.00	235,000	$117,500,000,000
	Totals:	150,062,000	$1,476,209,980,000

Now the estimates of each bracket were calculated the same way as the estimates with the current system. So assuming with the increase to the minimum wage, and there are approximately the correct number of taxpayers in each bracket, we can say **1.476** trillion dollars can be raised through the new income tax. With spending being **3.688** trillion in **2015**, we still need to raise a minimum of **2.212** trillion dollars.

In order to raise this tax revenue, this is where excise taxes will close the gap. As shown earlier the current system is antiquated and needs to be completely redesigned. First, all excise taxes must be percent based on product retail price. This will allow fair and uniform taxing on all products excised. Also for clarification, these taxes will be paid by the business or individual at time of purchase. Just like a state sales tax, businesses operating on US soil, must set aside the percent applied on the retail price for taxed products to be then collected by the IRS every month.

As opposed to the many categories with various tax rates that is in current use, my proposal will have seven product groups. The groups to be excised are: tobacco products, recreational marijuana products, alcoholic beverages, fossil fuels, firearms and ammunition, vehicles, and on all trades in US stock markets. In my proposal they will all have a tax rate of **25%** with the exception of stocks with a **5%** tax rate. It should be noted though that the tax rate on stocks would be applied to both the initial purchase of those stocks and when they are sold back.

Group	Products to be Taxed	Tax Rate	Estimated Income
Tobacco Products	Cigarettes, Cigarillos, Cigars, Chewing Tobacco, Loose Tobacco, E-Cigs and Vapor Accessories, Rolling Papers & Blunt Raps	25%	$25,773,000,000
Marijuana Products	Recreational Marijuana Sold Through Dispensaries, All Marijuana Edibles, All Marijuana Smoking Devices.	25%	$3,587,138,875
Alcoholic Beverages	Beer, Wine, and Liquor Sales Sold at Retail, Bars, and Resteraunts	25%	$18,675,000,000
Firearms & Ammunition	All Firearms & Ammunition Sold at Stores (In Store & Online) & Gun Shows	25%	$775,000,000
Vehicles	Retail Prices for Vehicles Bought, Leased, Rented & All Vehicle Parts	25%	$181,527,500,000
Fossil Fuels	Sale of all Fossil Fuels (Coal, Oil, Gasoline and Natural Gas)	25%	$48,617,250,000
Stock Market	Percent Tax on Purchase & Sale of US Stocks	5%	$3,150,000,000,000
		Total	$3,428,954,888,875

Math Shown on Page: 22

As seen at the bottom, the estimates accumulate to the amount of **$3.429** trillion. The majority of this coming from the implementation of a tax on every trade in US stock markets. According to the congressional budget office, as much as **$250** billion dollars is traded on an average day. With about **252** trading days in the year, that means about **63** trillion dollars is being moved annually. With a five percent tax, the IRS can bring in approximately **3.150** trillion. That alone almost pays for the entirety of government costs.

I am positive a tax like this will cause an uproar on Wall Street. Many investors would argue that this will hurt investment. In truth, a five percent hit both ways on an investment is not that much. For argument, let's say you invested **$100,000** into stocks of some company. You will pay the amount for the stocks and an additional **$5,000** in taxes to be collected by the broker or institution you are using. Total cost for those shares is now **$105,000**, plus any commission fees from the broker or institution. After three months in the market, perhaps those shares are now worth **$150,000**. If you go to sell those shares, the five percent tax on that is **$7,500**. The amount you receive back will be **$142,000** before any additional commission fees.

So for three months the *capital gain*, is **$37,000** after taxes are calculated totaling **$12,500**. Under the current system, these capital gains would be taxed at varying rates based on the investors tax rate, and weather the investment was held for a year or longer. For taxes sold under a year the tax rate is the same as the investor's tax bracket and the rate decreases after a year. Under this new tax system, there will be no capital gains tax as I stated earlier. It is only fair since the tax was paid before and after the investment that any further gain is yours to keep.

In a system such as this, it will not hurt investments. What will happen is an increase market stability. Since there are taxes on the front and back end of stock trades, it would be wise to hold these stocks longer to produce profits when selling. With less reckless trading it will reduce market volatility causing many of the modern economic troubles we experience. With the tax being done at the trade level, now all businesses and individuals will be taxed the same percentage based on their total investment and return.

The other major change in this tax plan, includes removing marijuana from the DEA's list of schedule one drugs. With public opinion in favor of legalizing and several states already doing so, it is time once again to end federal prohibition. It did not work with liquor in the beginning of the twentieth century, and with the prohibition of marijuana, it has led to the mass incarceration of millions of innocent people, and millions more that cannot obtain a decent paying job because of their "criminal" record.

It is only a matter of time before the right thing is done. An entire multi-billion-dollar industry has been forced underground to operate in the shadows. Once the federal government steps aside on this issue, states can then decide to boost their economies by regulating sales of marijuana. With that being said, for the states that have already decided to legalize recreational weed, then those sales should be taxed at a federal level.

For the year end of **2015**, Colorado had made almost **37** million dollars from a **10%** sales tax on marijuana. Just by that one tax alone, imagine it at a federal level. From my estimates it could be about **3.5** billion dollars. With this still being a new economy that is still growing with little financial data about it, this is the figure that is the most unknown. To calculate that figure, I used data from Colorado and Washington, the two states with the longest financial data on this industry. I started by finding the dollar value of money spent per person on marijuana. To do this I took the total sales in a twelve-month period and divided it by the state's population. With these averages, I then took the average of those two, and applied it to the US populous.

Until recreational use becomes legal across the nation, that would be the only way to truly determine the revenue produced. Including the fact that all smoking devices, and edibles would be taxed at the same rate will increase the tax revenue only further. Regardless of personal opinion on the use of cannabis recreationally, the question that has to be answered, does the government overstep through prohibition? When the *Twenty-First Amendment* was ratified repealing the prohibition of alcohol, the American people agreed then that the government overreached. It is time to undo one of the many mistakes of the past.

The reasoning for the taxes on these products is for three reasons. The first applies to the majority of these products being that they either cause health issues, or indirectly cause an increase in healthcare costs, i.e. the taxes on tobacco, alcohol, and marijuana. Think of it like this, in this system we have a single payer healthcare system. With a private insurer, they would ask if you smoked cigarettes. Those that did had to pay a higher premium. Well now that higher premium is the tax you pay on cigarettes. For vehicles and fossil fuels, these taxes are there to help pay for programs to counteract the climate change caused by those industries. For firearms, we all understand how these have increased healthcare costs.

The second reason, by making these all percentage based taxes, they can be applied simply to all products grouped in their industry. This allows for the same tax to now be fairly applied to tobacco products like cigarettes and chewing tobacco. Now before panic sets in for tobacco users and the industry as a whole; for a **$5** pack of cigarettes you would pay **$6.25** before state taxes are calculated in. The current federal excise is **$1.01** per pack which would total **$6.01** for the same pack.

Now for those who use chewing tobacco, a **$3.00** tin would now cost **$3.75**. To my knowledge currently, there is no federal tax on those tobacco products. Maybe taxes at the state and local levels, which is why the federal tax rates need to remain slightly lower to accommodate for the states to tax additionally as they see fit. Nevertheless, this specific change does not cause a drastic increase in price, and those who purchase these products will probably continue to do so.

That statement can be applied to all the products and stocks to be taxed in this new excise system. Every product listed is something that is federally regulated in one way or another currently. The difference is now all Americans would know why a product's price is higher than the retail price. Also all federal taxes are removed from the manufacturers and distributors if they were federally taxed before. This simplicity will alleviate a huge amount of stress from the IRS, and now allow them to focus on those who are avoiding taxes, or committing fraud.

The third and final reason for why this framework must be passed in a constitutional amendment is because this system now can begin to fund all necessary functions of government. The stock excise is the most important, and not only because it is the most profitable revenue source generating **$3.150** trillion minimum. It is important because this system removes the purpose of companies and those with wealth, hiding their capital gains in offshore bank accounts to avoid taxes.

More correctly though it is sort of a compromise, no capital gains tax on investments in return for steady taxes paid for the trades in US stock markets. If you still want to continue storing that money offshore then go ahead, but it is not helping the American economy. If you really like that bank's customer service, then it is your right to choose. What is important is no more tax evasion, and millions of wasted labor hours by the IRS trying to understand and enforce a **74,608-page** tax code.

For years, conservatives and anti-socialist agendas have tried to mislead the American populace that capitalism is the only viable answer to a successful America. That is just not the truth. They say social programs are bankrupting this country, when it has been the corporate welfare and crony capitalism that has stolen the country from the American people. With these two frameworks based off of preexisting powers by the constitution; we can raise a minimum of **$4.905** trillion. With a proper rework of programs, all citizens and taxpayers alike will finally be able to benefit from the taxes they pay for.

While its true capitalism does provide an environment for personal ambition to happen, it does not have the public's best interest at heart. As with any company the primary objective is to make a profit. For those who have medical bills, they need a health plan that will pay those bills when they are sick, not someone looking for a profit. The constitution already states the welfare of our nation must be provided for. Now that we know a feasible system with taxes can work, we can discuss how those funds would be spent.

In the next section we will discuss how a single-payer system can operate for everyone's benefit, and a redesigned framework for social security and disability. For our nation to move forward many changes need to be done, and must be done rapidly. With a new revenue of **$4.905** trillion, we must now look how all this can and should be used in a new budget, and start paying off the national debt.

Excise Tax Estimates

Tobacco Products: Calculated By Data From http://www.cdc.gov/tobacco/data_statistics/fact_sheets/economics/econ_facts/index.htm#sales

Individual Cigarrettes Sold (2015)	264,000,000,000	**Average Price Per Pack (Highest 11/2014)** $10.56			
Divided by Average Pack Size	20	**Average Price Per Pack (Lowest 11/2014)** $5.06			
Packs Sold (2015)	13,200,000,000 X	**National Average Price Per Pack** $7.81	= $103,092,000,000	**Est. Annual Cigarrette Sales**	

Est. Total Cigarette Sales $103,092,000,000	X	**25% Tax Rate** 0.25	= $25,773,000,000	**Est. Cigarrette Tax Revenue**

Marijuana Products:

States with Legal Recreational Marijuana 12 Month Sales

Populations as of 2016 Data From: suburbanstats.org

Colorado Legalised 11/6/2012	$313,226,353 ÷	5,029,196 =	**$62.28 Spent Per Person**

http://www.denverpost.com/news/ci_28947869/colorado-monthly-pot-sales-pass-100-million-mark

Washington Legalised 11/6/2012	$177,605,098 ÷	6,724,540 =	**$26.41 Spent Per Person**

http://dor.wa.gov/Content/AboutUs/StatisticsAndReports/stats_RMJTaxes.aspx

62.28 + 26.41 = 88.69 / 2
Average Amount Spent Per Person $44.35

http://www.census.gov/popclock/

US Population as of 5/2016	323,530,000 X	**Average Amount Spent Per Person** $44.35	=	$14,348,555,500 **Est. National Recreational Marijuana Sales**

Est. National Recreational Marijuana Sales	$14,348,555,500 X	**25% Excise Tax** 0.25	=	$3,587,138,875 **Est. Recreational Marijuana Tax Revenue**

Alcoholic Beverages

	Sales for 2015			
Beer, Wine and Liquor Store	$50,700,000,000 X	**25% Excise Tax** 0.25	=	$12,675,000,000 **Est. Retail Store Tax Revenue**

http://www.statista.com/statistics/197630/annual-liquor-store-sales-in-the-us-since-1992/

Bar Revenue	$24,000,000,000 X	**25% Excise Tax** 0.25	=	$6,000,000,000 **Est. Bar Tax Revenue**

http://www.statista.com/topics/1752/bars-and-nightclubs/
+
$18,675,000,000 **Est. Alcohol Tax Revenue**

Firearms & Ammunition

Calculated By Data From: http://www.cnbc.com/2015/10/02/americas-gun-business-by-the-numbers.html

Annual Revenue of Gun & ammunition stores	$3,100,000,000 X	**25% Excise Tax** 0.25	=	$775,000,000 **Est. Firearm & Ammunition Revenue**

Viehicles

Vehicles Bought (2010 Data)	$545,000,000,000 X	**25% Excise Tax** 0.25	=	$136,250,000,000 **Est. Vehicles Bought Tax Revenue**

http://www.statista.com/statistics/292474/revenue-of-new-car-dealers-in-the-us/

VehiclesLeased (2009 Data)	$109,000,000,000 X	**25% Excise Tax** 0.25	=	$27,250,000,000 **Est. Vehicles Leased Tax Revenue**

http://www.statista.com/statistics/295174/revenue-auto-leasing-loans-and-sales-financing-in-the-us/

Vehicles Rented (2015 Data)	$27,110,000,000 X	**25% Excise Tax** 0.25	=	$6,777,500,000 **Est. Vehicles Rented Tax Revenue**

http://www.autorentalnews.com/fileviewer/2230.aspx

Vehicle Parts (2009 Data)	$45,000,000,000 X	**25% Excise Tax** 0.25	=	$11,250,000,000 **Est. Vehicle Parts Tax Revenue**

http://www.statista.com/statistics/292522/revenue-of-auto-parts-stores-in-the-us/
+
$181,527,500,000 **Est. Vehicles Tax Revenue**

Gasoline

Calculated By Data From: http://www.statisticbrain.com/gas-station-statistics/

Gas Station Average Annual Sales $249,000,000,000	X (.5072 + .1487 + .0720 + .0531)	= $194,469,000,000	**Est. Annual Gasoline Sales**
(Sale Breakdown applied to Taxation)			
Unleaded Regular Gasoline 50.72%			
Diesel Fuel 14.87%			
Unleaded Mid-Grade Gasoline 7.20%			
Unleaded Premium Gasoline 5.31%			

Est. Annual Gasoline Sales $194,469,000,000	X	**25% Excise Tax** 0.25	=	$48,617,250,000 **Est. Gasoline Tax Revenue**

Stock Market

https://en.wikipedia.org/wiki/Trading_day

Average Value of Shares Traded Daily	$250,000,000,000 X	**Average Trading Days** 252	=	$63,000,000,000,000 **Est. Value of Shares Traded Annually**

https://www.cbo.gov/budget-options/2013/44855

Est. Shares Traded Annually $63,000,000,000,000	X	**5% Excise Tax** 0.05	=	$3,150,000,000,000 **Est. Stock Market Tax Revenue**

Universal Healthcare

The United States is long overdue for a rework of how healthcare is paid for. The system is antiquated, with no changes to its structure since the **1940's**. The system was originally made with the framework of capitalism in mind and how insurance policies work. A large pool of money collected by customers paying a monthly premium. Then if you need money in a situation for which your insured, then the insurance company pays all or a partial amount of the costs.

However, health insurance is unique from all other types of insurance. Car insurance is only necessary when you own a car. Rent or home insurance is only necessary when you are renting or own a home. Health insurance is the only type of insurance that every person will require from birth to death. While it can be financially crippling to not have any of these insurances when necessary, health insurance is the only one that not having can be fatal.

In the next section, we will discuss the current healthcare system, and the many systemic problems within. Once understanding those problems, a new healthcare system can be designed. It is time to create a system beneficial for all Americans, and remove the financial burden from both individuals and businesses.

Benefits of a Single-Payer System

Every time the subject of a single-payer system is brought up in discussion, it is usually dismissed immediately without any actual discussion. Usually it ends by someone saying it cannot be done due to cost or it is a socialist idea which would destroy America. For years this nation has been fed anti-socialist propaganda. The irony being this nation has had socialist policies since the **1930's**. With programs like *Social Security* and *Medicare*, this nation has already operated under a mixed economy of socialism and capitalism.

Many nations, including our closest allies like Canada, The United Kingdom, and Japan already have single-payer systems. With functioning tax revenues as shown earlier, the costs can be manageable. More importantly are the numerous benefits for every person and business in the nation once implemented. Once the benefits are listed and the costs proven, we can then start to shape what that system could look like in the United States.

Simplification is going to be the key to success. Since the idea is so quickly dismissed, the benefits are rarely discussed. Businesses will save money no longer needing to pay for health insurance. Healthcare providers will no longer have to worry if a patient's insurance will pay proper reimbursement of medical costs. Also the current thousands of healthcare plans will be replaced by one written by the *Department of Health and Human Services* (DHHS). Lastly, and the most important benefit, is now every person in the United States will finally have health insurance.

This will be a major change to how businesses offer competitive benefits for employees. For employers that currently offer health benefits, it accounts **7%** to **9%** of their total costs for employee compensation according to the *Bureau of Labor Statistics*.

Table A. Relative importance of employer costs for employee compensation. June 2013			
Compensation component	Civilian Workers	Private Industry	State and Local Government
Wages and salaries	68.5%	69.5%	63.8%
Benefits	31.5	30.5	36.2
Paid leave	6.9	6.9	7.3
Supplemental pay	3.6	3.5	0.8
Insurance	8.9	8.2	11.9
Health benefits	8.4	7.7	11.5
Retirement and savings	5.1	4.0	10.2
Defined benefit	3.2	1.8	9.4
Defined contribution	1.9	2.2	0.8
Legally required	7.6	7.8	5.9

Table From: http://www.bls.gov/news.release/ecec.nr0.htm

A company with a large workforce has to divert huge sums of money to pay for a competitive healthcare plan in addition to payroll expenses and taxes. Consider Walmart for example that currently employees **1.4** million people in the US according to their website. After the implementation of the ACA, Walmart and many companies in general have stopped offering health insurance to part time employees working under **30** hours. This is due to the ACA allowing more part time employees to qualify for Medicaid. Despite the ACA trying to improve the current condition, it created another unexpected consequence which has now become a burden. As stated from an article titled *Who Benefits more from Obamacare: Wal-Mart or Employees?* from *Corporation360*:

> *Obamacare mandates employer to provide a quality and affordable healthcare coverage to all full-time equivalent (FTE) employees. It also takes care of those left out of employer sponsored healthcare insurance. Looking at the opportunity to reduce cost, every firm including Wal-Mart, is now restructuring its workforce by cutting working hours of employees to reduce FTE workforce, as well as cutting benefits in compliance of the mandate.*

The consequence of the ACA is now many workers are forced into a ridiculous situation. With many employers only offering part time positions, this does allow those employees to qualify for plans offered through the health exchange. Unfortunately, these part time positions do not offer the payment needed to remain financially stable. This is why those with families to support, are often working two or three jobs, all of which part time, just to have enough income to provide food, clothing, and maintain the rent or mortgage payments.

For those in this position, the problem becomes that none of their jobs offer health insurance. Neither do those jobs provide enough income to afford private healthcare plans in addition to their bills. After all these are part time positions only paying **$7.25** to maybe **$10.00** if you are lucky. So if that is the case then those working part time can qualify for the exchange plans. Unfortunately, as too many Americans know, for those working more than one job, you end up making more income than the limit allowed to qualify for those plans. So what are you supposed to do when you do not make enough money to afford health insurance, but make too much money to qualify for health insurance under the exchange, and your employer no longer or never did offer health insurance?

By removing the ACA, government health programs and all privatized health insurance companies, no longer will anyone ever have to ask that stupid question again. By replacing these inefficient systems, employers can pay their employees a living wage, and those employees can use their income to live a sustainable life, and expand the economy. With employees making a proper wage working full time, those wages will then be taxed fairly to finance the single-payer health insurance program.

Next, let us discuss the current problems that face health care providers and pharmacies every day. Trying to bill insurance claims through all these different insurances has caused administrative burdens on healthcare providers. With the variety of healthcare plans in the country, there is very little consistency for what people will pay for procedures and medications, if their insurance covers any costs at all. These inconsistencies are both nightmares for the patients that require healthcare, but also for those providers trying to stay in business and receive a fair financial return for their product or services.

With consistency in reimbursements, the price for a majority of healthcare procedures and medications would probably go down. Hospitals and medical practices will no longer have to account for insurances not paying for procedures and medications for partial or all of the bill. Now as long as the practice has all their medical licenses up to date, and the patient medically needed the healthcare, then there will be no question in reimbursement.

The specifics of the billing in this system will be discussed later in this section. In brief, all bills that include physician prescribed treatments and procedures that would be reimbursed by private insurance companies; will instead be run against one of several plans written and financed by the federal government. These plans and payments will be run under the DHHS.

As with the IRS, this is another area of government in desperate need of help and reform. This is the department that currently oversees a majority of all social programs including *Medicare, Medicaid,* and *Social Security.* With the passage of the

ACA, the administrative burden for this group has increased just like the IRS. Now there are more health plans this branch of government must regulate in addition to everything that was already in place.

As I said simplification is key because government operates at peak efficiency when simple. Instead of the current thousands of pages in laws and regulations dealing with the many government health programs, it is replaced by one federal payment guideline used across US soil. Instead of medical providers or pharmacies adjudicating claims against the thousands of medical plans provided by companies like Aetna, or United Healthcare, now it will be run against the plans enforced by the *Department of Health and Human Services.*

In discussion of government run healthcare plans, many people fear that the government would control all aspects of healthcare. One such example is when Senator Rand Paul spoke in a subcommittee hearing **May 11, 2011**. During this hearing, the discussion of universal healthcare arose with the Republican senator saying, *"With regard to the idea of whether or not you have a right to health care, you have to realize what that implies… I'm a physician, that means you have a right to come to my house and conscripted me, means you believe in slavery."* He then goes on to say, *"If I'm a physician in your community and you have a right to health care, do you have a right to beat down my door with the police, escort me away and force me to take care of you? That's ultimately what the right to free health care would be."*

There are two very important distinctions that need to be discussed about the senator's remarks. The first is how in his assumption, he believes universal healthcare equates to all physicians are slaves, and their patients will use police to demand services. This is a ridiculous assumption. The reality is, when discussing healthcare as a right for all citizens by implementation of a single-payer system, government only takes over the role of insurance companies.

Healthcare providers remain independent as they are in our current system. They can still decide their prices and how those hospitals and practices are run. The difference is now instead of providers being reimbursed for their medical services by a mixture of private and government insurance policies, now all reimbursement will be done through one government policy.

The second point is where he states *"the right to free health care"*. No one has ever stated or argued that a single-payer system is free healthcare. As stated, this system is to be financed by taxpayer dollars. This means that instead of taxpayers paying some form of monthly premium or deductibles for their healthcare, the insurance is funded through collected tax revenue.

The biggest improvement is that all Americans would finally have health insurance. For those who have a vision of full health insurance coverage, that vision will only be reached by a single-payer system. Programs like the ACA and other patchwork in place will never allow for complete and total healthcare coverage in the United States. The only solution to ensuring complete coverage is by writing one healthcare plan for every citizen and legal resident.

In the current system there remain to many situations in which we can become uninsured. For approximately **49%** of Americans in **2014**, their health insurance was provided by their employer according to the *Kaiser Family Foundation*. At any time, employees can lose their coverage either through loss of their job, or if their employer terminates those plans due to rising costs. Regardless of the cause of loss of insurance, the transition period is often stressful, especially while needing a regular form of treatment or medication. The government has tried to place safety nets in place for this, however other problems have formed from this system.

Even if a person maintains health insurance, the change in coverage can be dramatically different. In some cases, a change in insurance can mean a change in prices for certain healthcare costs. Worst case scenario, your physician or local medical provider may no longer be in your plan's approved network. In this case you will have to pay the full price out of pocket, if that physician will still treat you.

In that same subcommittee hearing with Rand Paul, Debra Draper, Director at the *Government Accountability Office* was asked if it was true that if anyone needed medical assistance, could they walk into any practice and find a doctor. The question was asked by Senator Bernie Sanders, Independent from Vermont. It was asked in regards to Rand Paul's comments stating, "...*we have always provided* **100%** *access*" when discussing that physicians already provide universal coverage to all patients.

Debra Draper's response paints a very different picture: "*Well there's a huge body of literature that discusses the difficulties, particularly Medicaid beneficiaries had to finding of a physician. They're many physicians who are unwilling to accept Medicaid patients, and also for those who are uninsured face equally challenging or maybe more so challenging access issues.*"

In some cases, many physicians will not accept current government insurances fearing they will not get reimbursed. The difficulty to providers is despite they control the prices for their services, many do not know if they will receive proper reimbursement from their patient's insurance. For those who do not have insurance, many never get to see a doctor.

This nonsense would all come to an end. All medical providers will receive the proper payments for their services and every person will receive the healthcare they need. Never again will a medical provider have out of date insurance information. Never again, will a medical provider be outside an insurance's network and deny service to those who need it. Patients will never again be denied medical services that can save their lives, simply because they cannot afford it, or because of an untimely lapse in health coverage.

The Current Costs

While it is true healthcare costs are expensive, it is not impossible to fund a single-payer system. In the prior section we saw two important things. The first being our government already spends **1.028** trillion on healthcare in fiscal year **2015**. The second is that through a better taxation system like framework shown earlier, we can pay for any necessary increases. Not all politicians understand the importance of this issue though. For example, in a democratic debate on **February 11th 2016**, the following remark was said by Secretary Clinton, "*Health, this is not about math, this is about people's lives*".

While that is a great political answer to please people, she could not be more incorrect. I find this very worrisome due to the fact that to create a single-payer system, or any improved healthcare system for that matter, cost is the primary question. It is asked by those who are funding the program, and every American asking how much are they going to pay for their next prescription refill or procedure. For those without health insurance the weight of this question is huge. With a single-payer system then every US Citizen and legal resident can have the health care coverage they ethically deserve.

Many tax payers are being financially ruined by the privatized healthcare industry. The current healthcare system has become a burden to public good, and has allowed for the daily occurrences of corruption and fraud. If you have a good paying job, then yes, your employer may provide health insurance for you. However, this cost is a heavy burden to employers as well.

The current system is also a huge strain on state and local governments as shown earlier in the data table by the *Bureau of Labor Statistics*. To insure their workforce, **11.9%** of their total employee compensation was spent on health insurance. These private company costs have become a burden for the States as well as businesses and individuals. The current system taxes people and organizations multiple times for a completely inefficient system.

States for example pay costs associated to their employees' health benefits, but also for their portion of Medicaid programs they need to finance as the program is joint funded at the present time. Individuals are also paying split costs to a system in which a majority receive no benefit. Every tax payer pays **1.45%** of their income to cover costs of Medicaid. However, out of **150** million taxpayers, only about half or less qualify for Medicaid.

As showed earlier, the federal government spent **$1.028** trillion in **2015.** The state and local level governments spent **$574.2** billion and **$157.9** billion respectively that same year for a combined total of **$1.390** trillion dollars spent on healthcare by all levels of government. By removing these federal insurance programs, the States, and local governments will have an increase in unused tax revenue.

In addition to the over taxation for these inefficient health insurance products, for those that were uninsured at any time throughout the year, have had to pay a tax penalty since **2014**. Now that it is **2016**, the current penalty is the greater of either **$695** per adult or **2.5%** of family income. This is a terrible burden to have in place and only kicks people while they are already on the ground.

It is not that people choose to be uninsured; in most cases those who are uninsured are also unemployed or their employer does not offer health benefits. For those whose employer does not offer health benefits, it is usually the same employees making **$7.25** an hour. Even with the new exchange plans offered by the ACA, those trying to live on this wage cannot afford three meals a day let alone a **$30** a month fee for health insurance.

The ACA was meant to expand health insurance to Americans by creating subsidized plans based on income levels. These plans were to be offered by existing insurance companies already working with Medicaid accounts. The idea was that the more people who would enroll in the government option, the cheaper the plans would become and it would become self-sustaining.

Unfortunately, the whole entirety of the ACA is counter to its objective. The goal is to have everyone pay for health insurance, so that everyone is covered. Once everyone is covered, then it could be said in theory everyone can then afford any medical costs that come up. The incentive to get insurance is to avoid the fine if you are insured for any time for any reason. While the objective is the right idea, a single-payer system is the only one that can make this happen. Instead of some half-assed scheme, we could have just designed a single payer-system, insure everyone, and be done with it.

The reason that this was counterproductive is because insurance works by a large group of people pooling money together. Then as those who contribute need healthcare, some of those costs can be paid by that insurance company. The problem is that while you want competition to happen among health insurers to keep premiums low, in truth competition is doing the opposite. If you have more plans, but with less people paying into each of them, it is the reason why those insured have seen their deductibles and premiums increase.

The deductible cost must be paid before your insurance will actually cover any remaining costs on medical and pharmacy bills. What is the point of having insurance if you have to spend more money on health bills before your insurance will cover the costs? That is the whole point of health insurance!

This is one of the major problems many people face day after day. For those on exchange insurance, or lower tier health plans offered by employers often require this. Those families will not always have **$500** or **$1000** to pay up front for some procedure or medication before their insurance can help pay for it. Some deductibles cost even more than **$1000**. What is worse is all to commonly when an insurance company denies a request for a procedure or medication.

Sometimes insurance companies will want to know your entire health history, asking what prior medications or procedures you have tried. All because they are trying to save a couple bucks and want you to take a generic, or some cheaper alternative. Meanwhile the clock ticks away as someone is still waiting to get that surgery or medication.

For those who do end up using their health insurance, those health insurance companies are still making plenty in annual profits. The insurance company Aetna with total membership around **23** million, profited **$2.427** billion in **2015** according to their financial report. United Healthcare by contrast, the largest health insurer in the US with over **42** million insured, made **$5.868** billion that same year.

The total income from premiums for Aetna was **$51.618** billion and **$127.163** billion for United Healthcare. The total amount of revenue collected in premiums was only **$178.781** billion, which after operating costs still allowed those companies billions each in net gains. How is it that two companies insuring almost a fifth of our nation's populace, only pay out a fraction of the cost government pays on health care for over **65** million people, while a little under **40** million people still remain uninsured.

In addition, there are still over another hundred health insurance companies contributing in the private sector. On paper it looks like there is enough money and insurance companies to insure the entire populace twice over. However, middle-class and poor Americans are stuck in a system that does not function which most politicians will not acknowledge exists.

They think everything is fine and improving. Despite some drops in employer health coverage, health insurance companies have maintained the number of those insured or have increased due to health exchange plans funded by the ACA. Just because many Americans have insurance, does not actually mean they are fully insured for all medical emergencies. As discussed earlier, many Americans cannot afford any deductibles or out of pocket costs that are required to be paid first.

This system only grows more complex once you add in the multiple insurance plans, the many subsidiary companies involved, and third parties. The problem is private health insurers have created a bureaucratic mess in our healthcare system so they can profit. It is not that our government leaders are idiots and just accidently allowed this system to take place. Big insurers and big pharma have been buying elections since the sixties to make sure the system profits them.

So after reviewing all the angles of costs in this mess, let us get back to the original questions. What are the current costs of healthcare, and would the total cost of a single-payer healthcare system look like? The answer is not that simple when looking at all current health costs. Being most healthcare and prescription drug costs are inflated right now due to a corrupt system. The prescription drug industry is a prime example of the magnitude in which greed and corruption occur.

The most recent example being the public uproar after Martin Shkreli, former CEO of Turing Pharmaceuticals, who raised the price of the medication Daraprim. This medication treats parasitic diseases and is commonly used by patients with HIV. This has been on the market for sixty-two years, and until August of **2015** only cost **$13.50** per pill, or **$135** dollars per bottle of **100**. A day after Shkreli bought this medication, the price was raised to **$750** a pill or **$75,000** a bottle.

This is price gouging, plain and simple. What is problematic however, is that practices like this are not illegal. It is extremely immoral, but not every CEO of these pharmaceuticals are exactly motivated by increasing public health and your well-being. With a single-payer system, these pharmaceutical companies will no longer have the luxury to rob health insurance companies, when all reimbursements will be paid out by federal accounts. Under federal regulation, fair prescription drug prices shall be enforced.

When asking whether or not our nation should switch to a single payer system, it is not a question if the money is there to finance it. With all the wealth in our nation, the wellbeing of our populace should be a question of finance. The question is, do we as a nation have the courage to take the next logical and progressive step in history.

Fortunately for argument, the *Centers for Medicare & Medicaid Services* does keep track of all healthcare spending in the US. This being a group under the *Department of Health and Human Services*, they create yearly the *National Health Expenditure Accounts* that go back to **1960**. As stated by their website, they *are the official estimates of total health care spending in the United States*. For the year **2014**, these estimates totaled **$3.031** trillion. The next pie charts show where the money was collected from, and then how that money was spent.

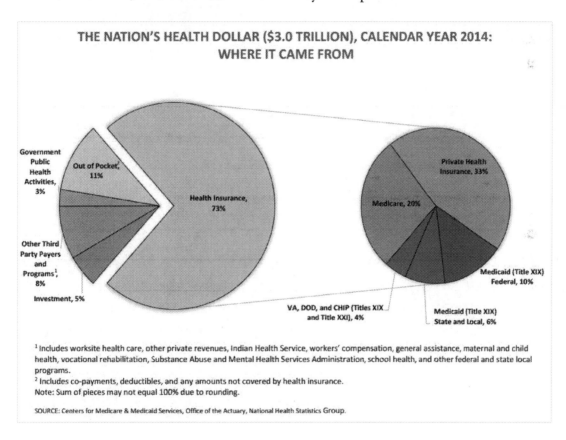

THE NATION'S HEALTH DOLLAR ($3.0 TRILLION), CALENDAR YEAR 2014: WHERE IT CAME FROM

[1] Includes worksite health care, other private revenues, Indian Health Service, workers' compensation, general assistance, maternal and child health, vocational rehabilitation, Substance Abuse and Mental Health Services Administration, school health, and other federal and state local programs.
[2] Includes co-payments, deductibles, and any amounts not covered by health insurance.
Note: Sum of pieces may not equal 100% due to rounding.

SOURCE: Centers for Medicare & Medicaid Services, Office of the Actuary, National Health Statistics Group.

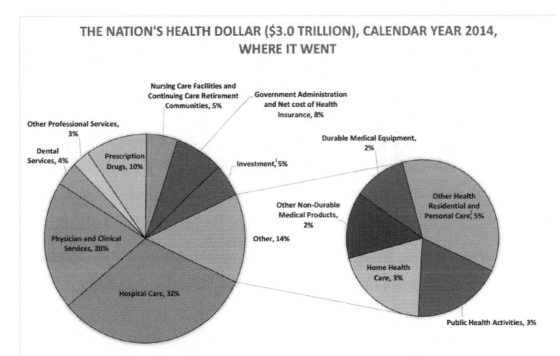

THE NATION'S HEALTH DOLLAR ($3.0 TRILLION), CALENDAR YEAR 2014, WHERE IT WENT

¹ Includes Noncommercial Research (2%) and Structures and Equipment (4%).
² Includes expenditures for residential care facilities, ambulance providers, medical care delivered in non-traditional settings (such as community centers, senior citizens centers, schools, and military field stations), and expenditures for Home and Community Waiver programs under Medicaid.
Note: Sum of pieces may not equal 100% due to rounding.

SOURCE: Centers for Medicare & Medicaid Services, Office of the Actuary, National Health Statistics Group.

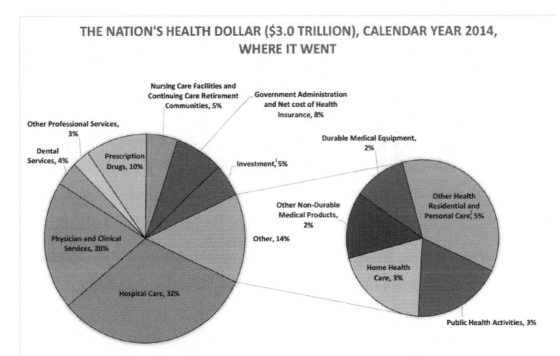

So in terms of a federal system, at current costs we would have to pay at maximum **$3.031** trillion, which is about three times the amount we are currently spending now. In comparison with the estimated tax revenue discussed earlier at **$4.905** trillion, there is a difference of **$1.874** trillion remaining to be used on other government departments and programs. Now current federal spending, with healthcare costs removed, remains at **$2.660** trillion the government needs to fund the remaining portion. In other words, at max cost we would be short **$786** billion.

Now in truth, a single-payer system in which everyone is insured, will probably not cost three trillion dollars. This is because that figure also includes all out of pocket costs paid by individuals, and investments in research and structures. As discussed earlier the high prices for both medications and procedures also impacts the bottom line, but would be difficult to calculate.

So the first thing to note is that as of **2014**, health insurance policies paid for **73%** or approximately **$2.213** trillion, of healthcare costs. Of that **73%**, only **33%** were payments made by private health insurance plans. The remainder came from government programs. This again makes me ask the question, why we are allowing private health insurance companies to profit billions, while the government is already paying for the bulk of healthcare costs?

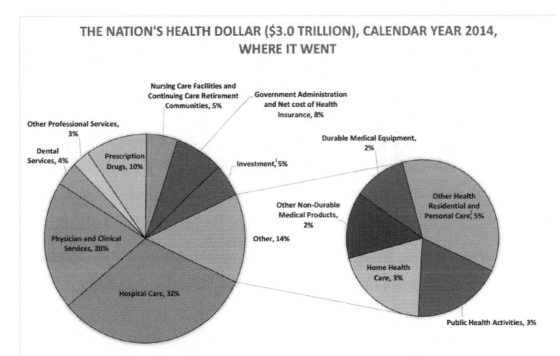

Once the government would begin processing all health insurance reimbursement, all *out of pocket* costs and the costs associated in that *investment* category would not be included in total cost. Therefore, in estimating the true cost, a single-payer insurance plan will only pay **84%** of the three trillion dollars, or approximately **$2.546** Trillion.

Now there is one other variable that has to be calculated in as well. That is the addition of healthcare payment for the approximate **30** million Americans who currently do not have health insurance. According to the same group *Centers for Medicare & Medicaid Services,* calculated that in **2014** healthcare spending was approximately **$9,523** per person. By multiplying that cost by the approximate number uninsured would equate to **$286** billion.

So with that plus the original estimate of **$2.546** trillion would total **$2.832** trillion. Before stating that this cannot be done, there are two items to keep in mind. The first being while the price tag of a single-payer system of **$2.832** trillion is high, is still leaves a remainder of **$2.073** trillion to fund the remainder of the federal government. Once the amendment is passed implementing a single-payer system, it would become the responsibility of DHHS to monitor health care spending, and incentivize practices to improve healthcare while lowering healthcare costs. This will be explained further in the next chapter discussing the framework and payment structure. Thus once everything is written and in place, the costs will probably be lower.

The second item to remember is that this is not the only program this arm of government oversees. As stated earlier they are responsible for payments to those qualified for social security and disability benefits. As shown in the last section when discussing the federal budget these two programs and other welfare programs totaled **$1.316** trillion.

Just as healthcare would vary in spending year to year, so do social security and other welfare programs. The other major issue over the last decade has been how to address the problems of *Social Security* as those getting paid out is growing faster than the amount being raised for the program. This will be discussed further in the next chapter, but here is the main idea.

The idea of this amendment is to get this nation moving forward again. If we are going to fix problems, it only makes sense to fix all the current problems. We cannot afford any more patchwork or band aids to keep stability. So with the implementation of a single payer-system, we can also rework the payment system of *Social Security* and *Disability.*

So when the budget becomes percentage based, a large portion of the budget will be for welfare programs. Now we must not think of welfare as a bad term and understand what this means. *Social Security, Medicare, Medicaid* and other welfare programs already accounted for **64%** of federal spending as of **2015**. Only now instead of the broken health insurance system, now we will have the program that may cost about **$2.832** trillion.

The question is now how much would a reworked cost of *Social Security* and *Disability* be? As stated earlier in **2015**, the current system paid **$1.316** trillion in a combination of those major and smaller welfare programs. Now in trying to estimate costs for these programs, once again they have the same recurring problem in government. Another complicated system that lacks logic. At the top of the next page is an example of how *Social Security* benefits are calculated for those who reach retirement age.

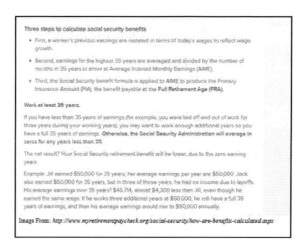

Now while this system sort of makes sense, it only gets worse and more confusing once you read the *Primary Insurance Amount* formula on the next page. Now I understand the idea the writers of this were trying to do. This takes in consideration your salaries over the years, and dependent on how much you put into the system then determines your return throughout retirement.

To put into terms of benefits it becomes further complicated. Once your benefit is calculated, then depending on your age you may only receive a portion of that income.

PIA formula bend points
The PIA is the sum of three separate percentages of portions of average indexed monthly earnings. The portions depend on the year in which a worker attains age 62, becomes disabled before age 62, or dies before attaining age 62.

For 2016 these portions are the first $856, the amount between $856 and $5,157, and the amount over $5,157. These dollar amounts are the "bend points" of the 2016 PIA formula. A table shows bend points, for years beginning with 1979, for both the PIA and maximum family benefit formulas.

PIA formula
For an individual who first becomes eligible for old-age insurance benefits or disability insurance benefits in 2016, or who dies in 2016 before becoming eligible for benefits, his/her PIA will be the sum of:
  (a) 90 percent of the first $856 of his/her average indexed monthly earnings, plus
  (b) 32 percent of his/her average indexed monthly earnings over $856 and through $5,157, plus
  (c) 15 percent of his/her average indexed monthly earnings over $5,157.

We round this amount to the next lower multiple of $.10 if it is not already a multiple of $.10.

Determination of the PIA bend points for 2016

Amounts in formula	Average wage indices		Bend points for 1979	
	For 1977	9,779.44	First	$180
	For 2014	46,481.52	Second	$1,085
Computation of bend points for 2016	First bend point $180 times 46,481.52 divided by 9,779.44 equals $855.54, which rounds to $856		Second bend point $1,085 times 46,481.52 divided by 9,779.44 equals $5,156.99, which rounds to $5,157	

Image From: https://www.ssa.gov/oact/cola/piaformula.html

According to the *Social Security Administrations* official site, **62** is the earliest a person can retire and begin receiving benefits, but it will only be **75%** of those benefits. The idea of retirement, from what I understood, is that when you become older and cannot work, social security is there as a safety net for older people to receive an income to maintain a stable life. Why allow people to retire, and receive benefits before the age of retirement? Sure it is a reduced amount of benefits they are receiving, but it undermines the whole damn purpose of a *retirement age*. Before reading into this, I had thought the retirement age, and thus the age to receive social security benefits was **65**. Turns out at that age you receive only **93.3%** of the amount. It is not until age **66** that you can receive the whole monthly benefit.

Here is now where this system gets worse. Benefits also take marriage into account. This is where our current *Social Security* benefits are further antiquated. Spouses only receive half of the benefit that their spouses would receive. Before age **66** they will earn even less than that. For example, if your age **62,** you only receive **35%** of that benefit amount. Considering when this was written, marriages were also understood as only being between one man and one women. Once again, even in our government policies, it says women deserve less money than men even in retirement.

In addition, many households now commonly have two major incomes regardless it be a traditional marriage or same sex marriage. Why should retirement benefits, or any government program be determined on marital status. Just like with the tax code and insurance, the importance of marital status needs to be removed from government programs. Once remove the system becomes fairer and easier to operate.

After all, marriage is a religious ideology, and while the constitution does not explicitly state the phrase *separation of Church and State*, our *Supreme Court* has always ruled in consistency with this ideology. The first amendment does protect freedom of religious practice to all people, therefore to remain impartial, the government should have full separation of Church and State.

So what would a social security program look like for America in the 21st century? To put in current perspective, once at age **66** assuming you were the working spouse, the maximum benefit is **$3,576** a month or **$42,912** annually. For retirement benefits that seems really high, especially considering that those that made six figure salaries over thirty-five years have earned millions in their lifetime.

Now for the majority of Americans though, that may only earn a million dollars in their whole lifetime, will only receive benefits around **$1,341** a month on average according to the *Social Security Administration*. What this equates to annually is **$16,092** or the equivalent of working **$7.73** an hour. It is a funny thing how the average benefits paid out is near the minimum wage. Just like the minimum wage, these benefits are not enough for seniors or anyone to survive with.

The reason why it is funny to me, is because my proposal is to link the minimum wage to be the same rate in which to pay out all beneficiaries on social security and disability. Instead of having that ridiculous pay scale depending on age, you raise the social security age to **70** and everyone will receive the same benefit. Of course for those about to retire soon, or already receiving benefits they shall continue to receive benefits and start receiving benefits at age **66**. Maybe word it that those born before **1970** can still retire at **66**, thus **1970** and afterwards cannot retire until age **70**. The reason being the average life expectancy for Americans is now in the mid to late seventies.

The important thing is now, regardless of marital status, or income throughout your life, you can now retire with dignity and receive an annual income the equivalent of the minimum wage. This also now allows for a simple payment plan to be developed in conjunction with the healthcare system run by the DHHS. The other benefit being that since this will now be a set payout system, beneficiaries can retire and start receiving benefits the day they turn **70**.

By using the minimum wage, that means they would make **$31,200** annually or **$23,400** after federal income taxes are applied which equates to **$1,950** in benefits a month, a **$609** increase to a majority of beneficiaries. This would now allow grandma and grandpa to retire at an appropriate age while receiving benefits to live the remainder of their lives with dignity. People who have worked their whole lives should not be forced to work part time at McDonalds or Walmart to help make ends meet.

So as with any discussion in changes to a program, what is the price tag associated?

https://www.ssa.gov/oact/STATS/OASDIbenies.html				
Account	**Those Currently Enrolled in 2015**	**Yearly Benefits**		
Social Security	49,156,959 X	$31,200 =	$1,533,697,121,000	
Disability	10,806,466 X	$31,200 =	$337,161,739,200	
	Total Payments	**Tax Rate**	$1,870,858,860,200	
	[$1,870,858,860,200]	X 0.25	= $467,714,715,000	Subtract Payment recollected through Income Taxes
Total Funds Needed For Social Security & Disability:			$1,403,144,145,000	

The total cost of a new *Social Security* and *Disability* program estimates at **$1.403** trillion. This added to the **$2.832** trillion being the estimate cost of a single-payer health care system means the total budget for the DHHS would be **$4.235** trillion. This leaves us approximately with **$670** billion to fund the remaining federal programs and bills totaling **$1.345** trillion.

This is a difference of **$675** billion. While this seems problematic, there are several factors that can make this system still balance out and still be able to fund all government programs. The first being the estimate cost of a single payer system. The cost (est. **$2.832** trillion) is most likely higher than the figure actually required. This does not take into account the money saved from reducing the administrative costs from multiple healthcare programs. Also mentioned earlier, was the fact that currently many medications and procedures are overpriced to currently maximize insurance reimbursements.

On the other side, the total revenue (est. **$4.905** trillion) is a very low figure in potential tax revenue. In all my estimates for the income taxes I used the minimum salary in that bracket and multiplied it by the number of citizens in each bracket. While the number in each bracket will probably be off in either direction, there is an unknown amount of revenue uncounted from each bracket. The most undervalued bracket would be the largest bracket (est. **130** million workers) being taxed at the **25%** level. This bracket ranged if your income was between **$31,200.00** (i.e. the minimum wage at **40** hours a week for **52** weeks) and **$99,999.99**.

It can be safely assumed many of the **130** million taxpayers will be making more than the minimum wage. The question is though how many workers and how much more? Until implementing a system like this, there are too many variables that will change in regards to an individual's income. I say this in a positive view because the variables will result in businesses being able to pay their employees more. Variables including the additional revenue businesses can redistribute to employees because they no longer have federal tax or health insurance expenses.

The other unknown is the reworks of federal excise taxes. This concept has many variables that can result in different levels of tax revenue. I do believe all of those estimates are undervalued because for a majority of all the products currently being sold, the sales data associated, range several years out of date. Also for marijuana for example, currently this industry is only legalized in four states, only two of which have sufficient sales data. This is another area where once the industry begins to prosper, the true tax revenue has unknown potential.

The largest potential is that of the tax occurred on every stock trade. Again the figure used was three years out of date. Therefore, the value of shares traded annually could be far greater than the estimated **$63** trillion. More importantly though is the fact that our nation is in a serious financial crisis being **$19** trillion in debt. The tax on stock trades could be potentially raised if more revenue is necessary without causing a big disturbance in the market.

For example, right now at a **5%** tax, the yield is approximately **$3.150** trillion. If everything else was the same and we raised the excise on stock trades to **6%**, the yield increases by **$630** billion dollars. Almost enough to cover the approximate differences if the other programs required every dollar estimated. The benefit of the new tax system is that the percentages can be raised or lowered to adjust the yields to balance the budget. It is time our tax dollars pay for our welfare, and not corporate welfare and corruption.

Framework for a Single-Payer System

After looking at all the costs associated, we can now discuss what a single-payer system looks like and how it could operate in **21ˢᵗ** century America. The first thing to understand is all the current entities in healthcare, and how a single-payer system will simplify healthcare for all those who provide and receive healthcare. Currently, there are several providers that provide thousands of health plans to individuals, families, and businesses.

These plans only get complicated further considering they may offer only a few of the several necessary health care services. Every plan should include medical, dental. vision, and prescription coverage. It is all too common though that if your plan does cover all areas, the deductibles are either outrageous, or your monthly premiums are through the roof.

This will be fixed by the DHHS writing one program for all healthcare providers to run claims against. With the program being funded by tax payer dollars, everyone in this nation will finally have health insurance, and providers will no longer have to worry about being reimbursed for their services. More importantly every citizen can then receive healthcare from any physician regardless of insurance provider or plan.

Now as stated current health plans are often written to specifically accommodate for smaller groups, often covering as little as possible to increase profits. The benefit of it being a government program is the DHHS only needs enough money to pay out for these programs, and operational costs. No longer would personal or government dollars meant for healthcare costs be used to provide billions in net gains for health insurance companies.

So what could one health plan look like by the federal government?

Group			Medically Necessary	Copay
Children < 3			100%	0%
Children 3 – 17			90%	10%
Adults 18 – 69*			85%	15%
Adults 70* +			100%	0%
US Veterans			100%	0%
Legal Residents & Tourists			80%	20%

	Medical Care	Dental	Vision	Pharmaceuticals
Medical Care Asscoiated with Attacks		100%		
Cancer & Emergency Outbreaks		100%		
All Birth Related Healthcare		100%		
Medically Necessary		Max %		
Coverage For Accidents		75%		
Cosmetic		0%		

(* age determined by the age allowed to start collecting social security benefits)

Considering most health care plans factor your age into determining your health care coverage, it only makes sense for the government to do the same. The difference being instead of a company trying to maximize profits, instead the plan has those covered in mind to provide affordable healthcare to all. It is for this reason why it makes sense for those who are most vulnerable, being the young and the old, to have all necessary healthcare covered by their plan.

For children under three and adults who have reached retirement age to register for social security, those are the citizens who deserve all health care coverage paid for. This now gives American parents a huge financial safety net while they are becoming parents for the first time, or adding another child. We have been constantly told by how politicians are pro family. Now it is time to see if these same politicians will support real change that is actually pro family.

Earlier when discussing the tax code, I stated that the new system removes all tax credits to simplify the system. I understand many will be outraged, (in particular those with higher incomes who hired accountants to make sure the receive every ridiculous tax credit). While that is true they are removed, several tax credits will still exist in different ways. For example, instead of seeing that tax credit for having children, now tax dollars collected will pay for medical costs for health care associated from a child's beginning during pregnancy, till they are three years old. This is something all American families will benefit from, and during a time of enormous stress to begin with, this is one worry the government can reduce.

Many politicians will say how they are pro family during campaign speeches and interviews. When it comes time to vote in Congress however, all of a sudden these congress members are not always voting the same way as they once promised. By supporting this amendment from the tax changes to the implementation of a single-payer system, they will be supporting the best pro-family legislation of all time.

As for those who reach the age of social security, it only makes sense any medical costs are completely covered. After all, that is the whole purpose of *Medicare*, the current program that pays *only some* medical costs for seniors. For most citizens at this point in their life, their only income is the benefits they receive from social security. That money should be used by them to pay their bills and enjoy retirement. Again they earned it, they worked their entire lives. As you get older, there will be more medical costs. That is just how it is. However, instead of an insurer denying payment for a procedure or medication to a senior, now the government plan will just pay the cost, end of story.

As long as the physician is not committing fraud, then it should be trusted that the treatments ordered by the physician is for the patient's best interest. This ideology is to be applied to all areas of healthcare for all patients. The most important being pharmaceuticals. Out of all avenues of healthcare, pharma is by far the most corrupt, and where the most money is being wasted.

The reason for this is because of third party payers called *Pharmacy Benefit Managers* or PBMs. The current system for someone to receive a medication is not simple at all. We all understand that for patients to receive a prescription from a pharmacy, the physician needs to write a prescription for it. In this step alone, millions of American's run into problems already affording this prescription because either they do not have health insurance, or their local pharmacy is not in their health insurer's network.

For those who are in the network, the cost for that medication may be covered to an extent. The cost of course will vary depending on the plan and if there are deductibles. Where the headaches begin for all parties, i.e. the patients, physicians, pharmacies, insurance companies, and PBM's is when any healthcare requires *Prior-Authorization*. What this means, is that before a patient can receive any healthcare, there is a process that must be completed to ensure the patient deserves this healthcare and to what extent the insurance company will pay.

Before working in the healthcare industry, I had assumed that if a physician had written a prescription, all health insurance companies would acknowledge the healthcare was necessary and therefore should be covered. Speaking in terms of prescriptions, many medications that are expensive and often brand name will not be covered unless a patient has tried several cheaper generics first.

My tenure at a pharmacy called *Philidor Rx Services* is what introduced me to the soul crushing reality that is our corrupt healthcare system. For those who read business articles during October and November **2015**, then you are familiar with the fact this pharmacy was associated with scandals and fraud with its "parent company" *Valeant Pharmaceutics*. The reason for quotation marks there is because legally Valeant never owned Philidor. Valeant had only paid **$100** million to Philidor for an *option to buy it*. It is through this agreement that Philidor's relation to Valeant was that of a *Variable Interest Entity* (VIE).

A *CNBC* article from **October 22ed, 2015** titled, *Are Valeant, Philidor, and R&O all the same company?* explains this agreement as, *a company that holds a VIE generally enjoys exposure only to the upside of its results, or only to its downside, or it directs the actions of the company.* In the case of the Valeant-Philidor relationship, Valeant experienced all three of these criteria. The legal problem that arises from a VIE is that the parent company can consolidate the VIE company's finances into their own.

This is what began the problem when investors began asking questions to Valeant executives wondering how the stock price doubled in **2015** from its value in **2014**. Once ties to Philidor came to light, the shady business practices of Philidor also came to light. As stated Valeant's stocks doubled in price from the creation of Philidor locate in Pennsylvania and the pharmacy network it created through acquisitions like that of *R&O Pharmacy* in California. It was these shady business practices that resulted in Valeant's stock price to dropping from **$263.79** a share at its height in August **2015** to around the high twenties to low thirties it fluctuates at now.

What Philidor did was that it was a cross between a *specialty pharmacy* and a *mail-order pharmacy*. It operated in a legal grey zone to provide Valeant's products to consumers at a cheaper price while bypassing the prior authorization process that many insurers required for Valeant's dermatological products. The primary product being the medication Solodyn, which is popular for treating *Acne Vulgaris*. However, many insurance companies, and consequently the contracted PBMs that handle the pharmacy benefits require that patients have tried at least two generics before using Solodyn as thirty pills cost a little over a thousand dollars. This was bypassed since the pharmaceutical company was working with the pharmacy. Valeant would provide coupons to move the product for only **$35** if insurance didn't cover the medication

The purpose of Philidor was to expose a cash flow from insurance companies. For the plans that did cover these overpriced, and often medically unnecessary medications, Philidor and Valeant profited. Meanwhile, for the medications not covered by insurance, employees like myself in the *Prior Authorization Department* tried to get those medications approved by the insurance company.

The job in this department consisted of sending the necessary paperwork associated with the PA process to the physician. While this sounds simple enough to accomplish, this is where the limbo can begin for many patient's prescriptions. The paperwork sent to the physician had to be the form used by the correct PBM that is currently contracted with that patient's insurance provider. For example, if a patient has health insurance from *United Healthcare*, the PBM associated with them is *Optum Rx*. On the other hand, some insurers like *Aetna* review all prescription claims themselves directly.

Where it gets further complicated is that many of these insurance providers contract through several PBMs. In order to operate in many states, insurance companies will contract with different PBMs already legally licensed in certain states. Normally the physician is the one required to handle the prior authorization process, but that was the point of Philidor.

Our goal was to reduce the administrative burden on physicians by sending them the necessary paperwork. Once they filled it out, they could either send it back to us, or directly to the PBM to review it against their formulary to see if a patient has met the criteria for the medication to be covered. This is where we ran into one of several problems. The headache occurs because physicians do not want to do this paperwork. In all honesty, they shouldn't have too. If they are prescribing a medication for the patient's best medical interest than it should be covered.

For the physicians that do play fairly in the current system, further confusion can occur in this process. As stated sometimes a patient's insurance plan can be unclear as to who is supposed to review the benefits for a patient's insurance. When working at Philidor, several times when I would call an insurer such as *Blue Cross and Blue Shield of Texas* and ask for them a status check on a claim for a patient, they would tell me they don't review that patient's specific plan and that another PBM like *Express Scripts* or *Prime Therapeutics* would review their benefits.

Once hanging up I would then call the next company to only then be told that the previous company I hung up with is the one who reviews that patient's benefits.

There were hours of my life wasted on these phone calls going back and forth trying to get a status check of a claim submitted so a patient can begin a medically necessary treatment.

Physician's run into the same problems when they try to reach out on a patient's behalf to expedite the system. Other problems include when a patient's insurance changes. So much time was wasted when we were trying to run a claim against a patient's insurance, when in actuality that insurance info may have been several years out of date and was never updated by the physician or patient. It is for this reason when patients have a continuing therapy, many times their therapy can be stopped if their insurance changes. This being whether a patient's new insurance now requires prior authorization or does not cover the medication altogether. Also new insurance can mean a new deductible that has to be paid first as well.

On the other hand, some pharmacies are able to expedite this process because some pharmacies and PBMs are owned by the same company, and thus can review the claim against their own formulary at the same time when trying to fill the prescription. *CVS Pharmacy* is an example of this because of their PBM *CVS Caremark* which has spent years contracting with every major health insurance group to be in their network to thus have medications filled through their pharmacy efficiently.

As you can imagine, this is of course an unfair advantage for some pharmacies, and limits choice for consumers. Under the new system it still makes sense to say certain prescriptions should be preferred in treating certain illnesses. However, patients do not have the time to wait weeks or even months to find out if their insurance will pay for a medication they desperately need.

So under this new system, pharmaceuticals will follow the same payment plan as shown in the second chart. For medications medically necessary they will be covered to the max percent depending on the patient's age. The DHHS can record which medications are to be approved for what purposes and should work with physicians and pharmaceutical companies to define this list. Therefore, any medication prescribed for a preapproved diagnosis will be covered no questions asked assuming the physician is in good standing with the local, state, and federal governments.

What this equates to is creating price transparency in the healthcare system. A fear of this idea is that it will lead to an increase in healthcare costs. This being that if patients know that the cost of their treatment will be zero, they will pick the more expensive option thinking it will provide better results. To this thought, why would patients be choosing their treatment?

The whole point of seeing a physician when sick is to consult their opinion in order to be healed. Therefore, it should only be the physicians choosing what medication or procedure for the patient based on their medical judgment. Again, physicians will have to make decisions based on what they feel is the best treatment for the patient, and should no longer have to worry about if the patient's insurance will cover such a treatment.

By allowing this, the DHHS can work with physicians to decrease medical costs over time. Since physicians can now give the best treatments and surgeries to patients, we can now focus healthcare to cure ailments. This would be a large improvement over the current system in which pharmaceuticals only design treatments in which create more money as long as insurance companies will continue to pay. With one insurer, the focus can now be changed and pharmaceuticals will have to oblige or go out of business.

Going back to the chart earlier, for kids **3-17, 90%** of their medical costs would be covered and for those **18-69, 85%** is covered. The reason for this is because during these ages healthcare is often at its lowest, and this is the age range in which you are working a full time job, thus able to help pay for any medical costs in addition to yearly checkups.

Where this system improves our nation further is we finally solve two problems that should have been addressed far earlier. The first being all United States veterans will now have all medically necessary healthcare completely covered. From the day you sign up till the day you reach retirement age, all **100%** of healthcare is covered. The only reason a veteran would not have these costs completely paid for is if they were dishonorably discharged.

We have all seen the failure of the *Veteran's Affairs* to provide proper health insurance to our veterans. The main problem goes back to the fact that many physicians and pharmacies were not in the network of the VA. For this reason, many veterans have been denied healthcare, by not being close enough to a physician in their network, or the VA not covering the healthcare due to cost. After serving our country, especially many returning after several active combat tours in the past twenty years; there is not one valid reason that their nation cannot pay for the healthcare of those who allowed us to live our lives the way we do, every day.

Now this is not to remove the VA, they still have a purpose and can still help veterans with education, and providing good loans for homes and cars. In terms of healthcare though, we have seen them fail, and those who have served this nation should suffer no longer. For those who put themselves on the front lines, paying for their healthcare is the least we can do to repay their service.

The last group is those who are here as legal residents (those with green cards and work visas) and tourists in this nation. This is one reason why tourism in the US has dropped over the years. As stated many industrialized nations have some form of universal healthcare in their nations with many operating under a single-payer system. This meaning that if you are visiting a foreign nation with this system, and become ill or get hurt while oversees, then their government system will cover a portion of your healthcare bill.

Meanwhile if any tourist in the US gets hurt or becomes ill, and goes to the hospital, they can be financially ruined. Many tourists that came to the US, will commonly purchase a health policy from an insurance company before visiting to avoid that risk. The truth is that is absolutely ridiculous. Those who are legal residents paying income taxes in the US should also receive a fair benefit in return. The obvious difference being only **80%** of costs will be covered regardless of age.

Now, to explain the next chart, these are the six categories in which healthcare is often required. The first three would have all costs associated completely covered. *Medical Care Associated with Attacks* includes attacks from people such as a terror attacks or mass shootings for example. One recent congressional battle was that of the *Zodroga Act*, which was legislation that provided health benefits to first responders of *9/11* that developed health complications. At the end of **2015**, this legislation was going to expire if congress did not renew it. John Stewart, who after retiring from the *Daily Show*, had brought awareness to this issue to help ensure it passed.

While the idea is a positive and good natured one, it saddens me that we still had to argue that those who helped in this terrible disaster deserved health insurance benefits. This simply should not have been an issue; which is why it will now be included in the health insurance program. Those either in the disaster, or those who were helping in the aftermath, should have all healthcare associated with that disaster covered. This also applying to those who require healthcare after natural disasters such as a hurricanes or tornados.

Under *Cancer & Emergency Outbreaks*, any and all diseases should be matched up against the best medications, treatments, and medical equipment we have in this nation. The reason this is not currently done is many insurance companies want to increase profits, and you cannot do that when you are paying out thousands of dollars for cancer treatments. This is again why health insurance as a business directly undermines its sole purpose which is to pay claims for when beneficiaries get sick.

Medical outbreaks like *Ebola,* that happened a few months back, and currently the *Zika Virus* that is causing problems in South America require large amounts of financial resources. What makes diseases like these horrifying is how rapidly they can spread, and the increase in medical costs associated. Especially in terms of *Zika*, which has now infected citizens on US soil. Considering that diseases like these and Cancer will not discriminate if your young, old, black, white, rich, poor, gay, straight, citizen or visiting from another nation. For this reason, it is not only ethically fair, but a moral obligation to not discriminate health insurance for all those who require it to fight these diseases.

Lastly in the **100%** covered groups is all costs associated with childbirth. This includes ultrasounds during pregnancy through the hospital costs of the baby's birth. As stated in the new tax system, there would be no tax credits. It is not to say they have been deleted, but rather reutilized in better ways. Instead of families trying to get money back from taxes to pay for bills, now they can focus on their bills, and not worry about medical costs for their children. No longer will new families feel the burden of being underemployed with no health benefits. We can once again give our citizens a system in which to survive.

Now there is one thing to note though about these three groups. That is that the healthcare costs covered apply to both citizens and all legal residents and tourists. It is only ethical to do so, none of these people planned for these circumstances to take place and require health care. This is the same reasoning for cancer and all severe medical outbreaks. These problems are not planned, and it only makes sense to make sure these costs are covered as opposed to bankrupting our people.

So now the next group is the percentage paid for all medically necessary treatments and procedures. The costs of this will vary depending on your age as a citizen as shown in the first chart. For all legal residents and tourists, your amount covered is **80%** of the medical costs regardless of age. This is to be for all regular checkups, medications and procedures as are required throughout life.

As to what the specifics of the plan are, that will have to be written by the DHHS. For those with insurance, it will not be much different than the guidelines used by your current insurer. The difference now is that once the government would become the payer for all, healthcare will improve and everyone will have access.

The largest improvement would be in regards to pharmaceuticals. With costs no longer being an issue, physicians can prescribe patients the medication they need, and as long as that medication is an approved treatment for the diagnosis provided, then no more will patients have to worry about a prior authorization process. In regards to the pharmaceutical companies, their jobs will become easier as well. In the current system, these companies waste millions of dollars in advertising, and trying to have physicians prescribe their medications.

A new deal can now be made between these pharmaceuticals, the DHHS, the FDA, and the physicians. Currently, all medications have to be approved by the FDA to be allowed for use in US markets. Additional criteria can now be added by the FDA when approving medications. For example, if pharmaceuticals want to release new medications that would compete against something already existing; it only makes sense now to request that it is either the same price, or even lower.

Naturally this assumes the new medication and existing have equal treatment capabilities. The point is now we can focus pharmaceuticals to decrease costs of their medications to compete with existing products. The trade is the benefit they receive considering once a medication is approved by the FDA, that medication can then be simultaneously added to the DHHS drug formulary that is to be referenced by all physicians nationwide.

No longer would drug manufacturers now have to prove their case to every insurance company to add their medication and cover it under any number of their plans. Now if the FDA approves it, that is the benefit of there being only one health insurance as another branch of government. Those in the FDA can then contact those in the DHHS and state what diagnosis the medication is good for. Thus now in one day, a new medication can be approved and be allowed on the market nationwide immediately.

It would now be the job of that pharmaceutical to convince physicians that their medication would treat their patients better than the current product. What remains important in this system is that physicians and patients can agree to the best treatment or medication to help them. Instead of insurance companies forcing physicians to use cheaper alternatives, physicians can now recommend all options, and every patient no longer has to worry about a majority of the cost.

There will be a common argument raised here, suggesting that this would lead to the cost of higher medications and treatments being chosen by patients. Thus causing the cost of the program to be inflated. As stated previously, there is to be a trust with physicians. All physicians in order to operate in the United States have to register and obtain a *National Provider Identification Number* (NPI). All costs will be reported to the DHHS. If there are any irregularities or showings of fraud, those physicians can then face penalties including their NPI revoked, fines, and imprisonment. Also, if there are any pharmaceuticals try to raise prices again like Martin Shkreli with Daraprim, those responsible should be charged with price gauging as this was, and face federal imprisonment.

Additionally, to keep costs down, that is the reason for the final two categories *Accidents* and *Cosmetic*. Accidents being **75%** of costs covered would include incidents such as breaking a leg skateboarding, or equivalent medical treatment for something self-caused. This percentage being the same for those who are not citizens since it is less than the **80%** rate.

Secondly, any medications or procedures that are strictly for cosmetic use, nothing is to be covered by taxpayer dollars. The purpose of health insurance is to help pay for medical costs for those who are not planning on spending their income on these bills. Therefore, if you want that Botox or lipo surgery, then you pay full price. This way all areas of healthcare are now covered under one plan for everyone, without finances being wasted on elective procedures.

So we see how this benefits the federal government, the people, the physicians, pharmacies, and pharmaceutical companies. The final group this benefits is every state and local governments. As the plan shows, this is completely financed by taxpayer dollars, and operated by the DHHS. The state and local governments can now rebudget the amount of money originally left aside for their share of Medicare and Medicaid.

On top of that, the states also no longer have to haggle with health insurance companies and pay premiums for their employee's year after year. There is only one group that does not benefit, and that is obviously the health insurance companies. Yes, they would be put out of business. While there would be many people put out of work, there are many work projects this nation needs to do and quickly. Projects such as fixing our crumbling infrastructure, and investing more resources into the increased development of solar panels, and other renewable energy sources.

So that leaves us with one final question. How does this payment system operate on a consumer use level? This is where innovation is going to have to come into play. The first thing to remember is that the DHHS under this new system would oversee and pay for three programs. These being the single-payer system, Social Security, and Disability in addition to its own operational costs. It is time for every US citizen to receive a new and updated social security card.

Imagine, just like how credit cards now have chips in them that process transactions; we could now implement the same technology into a new social security chip card. For every citizen who receives medical treatments, licensed physicians should have machines that can read these cards to submit the invoices to the DHHS. As for those who are tourists, or are living here legally will have a similar green card that will also have a chip.

It is these two cards that will allow for this healthcare system to work. Basically these operate as a cross between a credit card, and a state ID or driver's license. Since this will be a new legal ID, the patient's age information would always be associated to their account, thus determining the proper co-payment. In the last chapter of the final section, I will discuss more in detail on the new social security cards and green cards, and how we go about implementing it.

A New Deal for Businesses

In this section, I will now discuss in further detail of how businesses will operate with all the changes discussed to this point. For there to be a successful economy in any nation, there must be a healthy relationship between businesses and the government. In successful nations, they have provided environments in which businesses had the freedom and opportunity to expand and prosper.

Throughout history, part of this relationship was the agreement to how far an employer had to protect and provide for workers, and at which point is the government overstepping. The United States, which only began **240** years ago has never been a nation to truly lead the fight for actual freedom. Slavery did not end until **December 6ᵗʰ 1865** under the *Thirteenth Amendment.* The fact **151** years later, racism is still a prevalent part of our society is only further shameful.

To move forward, our nation must allow every citizen equal opportunity to succeed to the level of their own ambitions. A wage of **$15** an hour is nonnegotiable being the minimum amount of money a person needs to earn to live. For those in the business world afraid of this being a disaster, I will prove how this will lead to unprecedented economic growth. It is time to implement part two of the new deal. Learning from our past we will not repeat the same mistakes.

No Federal Taxes on Businesses

Every business in the United States agrees the current tax system is hurting economic growth, and even the cause for companies moving oversees. One reason includes the burden presented from FICA Taxes. This is the tax that in effect punishes employers for hiring large number of employees and paying them well. This is because for the portion of an employee's pay that gets withheld for Social Security and Medicare taxes, the employer must match those amounts equally.

Even for large companies earning billions in yearly revenues, the higher the wages they pay, the higher the FICA taxes they must also pay. Consider Walmart with **1.4** million employees, they need to earn enough revenue to pay those employees, while affording their FICA contribution in addition to remaining operating costs. Currently most American Walmart employees are now paid around **$9.00** an hour starting. While it is noble of them to have a higher wage than the minimum wage, it must be pointed out that a majority of their employees are part time, only working about **34** hours a week. The following breakdown shows the estimates for the payroll expense and FICA tax expense on any given year for Walmart.

Current Walmart Payroll Expense Estimate					
	Average Wage	Average Work Week			
Average Wage:	$9.00 X	34 =	$306 X 52 Weeks = $15,912	Annual Payroll	
Annual Expense For	Employees	Annual Payroll			
Workforce:	1.4 Million X	$15,912 =	$22,276,800,000	Minimum Employee Payroll	
		FICA Taxes	7.45%		
			$1,659,621,600	Employer FICA Tax Contribution	
		+			
			$23,936,421,600	Total Employee Expense	

It costs Walmart approximately **$1.660** billion in additional revenue to pay for its workforce in the United States. This cost in addition to all other federal and state taxes have become a crippling burden. This is equally a burden on small stores because this is a percentage based tax on current payroll expenses. One reason why companies cannot hire more people occasionally is this tax alone. So, what would it look like under the new tax system with a **$15.00** minimum wage?

New Walmart Payroll Expense Estimate						
	Minimum Wage	Average Work Week				
Average Wage:	$15.00 X	40 =	$600 X 52 Weeks = $31,200 Annual Payroll			
Annual Expense For	Employees	Annual Payroll				
Workforce:	1.4 Million X	$31,200 =	$43,680,000,000 Minimum Employee Payroll			

Assuming a majority of their workforce returns to full time, naturally this will be an increase in a business's payroll expense. To be expected, I am sure many people are now skeptical of how raising the minimum wage can be financially sustainable. Just at minimums for payroll expense, it is true in the case of Walmart, the expense would be increased by about **$20** billion. However, this is still easily affordable considering three important factors.

The first being as stated, no business that operates on US soil will face federal taxes other than any charges associated to the purchase of an excised product. State and local taxes will still be applied based on their individual laws. This should increase competition between states and localities within to create better tax systems to attract more businesses to operate in their jurisdictions. The responsibility to create businesses, and ensure they can succeed to employ the millions of people in our country that want jobs is shared by all levels of government, and the private sector.

Secondly, healthcare is removed as a requirement for employers to offer to all full time employees. Walmart and every other company no longer has to provide healthcare to their employees. By removing this burden, companies can go back to offering full time positions at better wages.

The final point being Walmart's net income in **2014** was still a little under **$27** billion after all expenses paid according to their financial statements. Like most large corporations, they are making more money than what they are sharing with their employees. Also if some prices have to be raised, then so be it. For smaller businesses, and particularly fast food businesses, this will have to occur. For the most part, at most you will see some products go up a dollar. Instead of buying that cheeseburger of the dollar menu, now it might be two bucks.

I believe some progressives will be angry that businesses will not receive a federal tax. Most likely arguing that if businesses are not paying taxes, they are not doing their contribution to society. In actuality, the greater contribution businesses provide is the paychecks earned by their employees. It is this social contract that allows goods and services to be provided for the populace, and allows those who produce these to also purchase them.

It has been our consumer culture that has provided our economic growth since World War II. When there are enough jobs to provide stable incomes to a populace, that populace then gets to participate in the economy and purchase those goods and services. We need a system in which this economy can exist again. Currently too many Americans are struggling just to pay their bills, let alone participate and spend money in our sluggish economy.

With more citizens earning income, more businesses can grow and increase their services. We can begin steady economic growth again, as opposed to our current cycles of slight growth, then narrow avoidance of economic disaster. In the next chapter I will prove why **$15.00** an hour is necessary and not an ungrounded demand.

In regards to the overall budget of the US, there are two things to remember. Federal revenue from corporate taxes in **2015** totaled **$343.8** billion. The total collected for social insurance taxes which include FICA totaled **$1.065** trillion. This tax is split between the employer and the employee. Therefore, it is safe to say that half of this was collected from businesses equating to **$532.5** billion. In total, **$876.3** billion were collected from taxes on businesses in **2015**. I would argue that money is better utilized by these businesses to increase their payroll expense so that no one makes under **$15.00** an hour.

This is the new deal. The federal government will not tax any legal business in exchange for setting a proper minimum wage that all business must obey to legally operate. As shown a living wage only equates to **$31,200** gross pay. After taxes an employee will take home a salary of **$23,400** every year. With everyone earning this whom works a *Full Time Equivalent* job, at a minimum the government is collecting **$7,800** per year in income tax.

While I am confident this increase in the income tax would cover the losses from no FICA and corporate taxes, I do not have the time to begin calculating what that difference would be considering all the variables. What can be calculated though, is the minimum increase in income taxes by getting the approximately **8.297** million people employed that are currently unemployed according to the *Bureau of Labor Statistics*. The how will be discussed in the last chapter of this section. If all of them were employed earning at least the new minimum wage working forty hours a week, that means the income tax would bring in an additional **$64.717** billion.

Even if the income tax does not end up making the difference from no businesses taxes, the excise tax on stock trades will definitely cover the difference as discussed earlier. As estimated, it could bring in about **$3.150** trillion while not hurting investment. I understand the original skepticism that arises from the discussion of a tax on stock trades. It has to be remembered though that capital gains are no longer taxed. This applies to both individuals and businesses that invest in stocks.

While this will probably increase gains for those investors, it more importantly simplifies the system for the IRS. The only work the IRS now has to do is verify W-2 records from businesses against everyone's social security number for citizens, or legal resident number for foreign workers. Now when looking at the books of different companies, all they will have to do is compare the records of payroll expenses to an employee's income. As long as those numbers are being reported correctly then everything is fine. As far as the excise taxes go including those on stock trades, as long as the industries hold aside the proper amounts for taxes, then they can continue to legally operate. Now if there is fraud, or numerical discrepancies, the IRS can now focus on these crimes, as opposed to investigating whether you have two or three kids, and when your divorce was.

In all honesty though, this only works by implementing every change as discussed thus far in a constitutional amendment. The US people are hurting and need a good economic system to provide good paying jobs. We need a proper tax system in order to allow this economic system to function. In addition, we also need a single-payer healthcare system to allow fair treatment to all people in the US. Again though, this can only occur by implementing a proper taxation system. Thus once all this is put in place, government, businesses and individuals will all benefit.

$15.00 An Hour Minimum Wage

Throughout the primary election, there has been a recurring rally cry referred to as the *Fight for 15*. This is the idea that all workers deserve a living wage. The movement believing that this living wage equates to **$15.00** per hour of labor provided. Many groups and individuals have come out against such an idea, the majority opposition reason being it is too radical and unsustainable. Not only is a raise to the minimum wage long overdue, **$15.00** is absolutely necessary for anyone to maintain a stable life.

The minimum wage began in **1938** as part of the new deal legislation signed by President Roosevelt. Originally it was **$0.25** an hour and has been raised many times since. In recent history, as of **1997**, it was set to **$5.15** an hour. It was not until **10** years later in **2007** that is was raised again to **$5.85**. The minimum was then raised again in both **2008** and **2009** to **$6.55** and **$7.25** respectively. This now being the current minimum wage we have today. On **July 24**th this year, it will have been **7** years since the bottom floor has been raised.

The whole purpose of the minimum wage was to eradicate poverty from the United States. With everyone earning a living wage, those working could then participate and expand the economy. Despite wages remaining stagnant for near a decade, inflation does not stay the same. For this reason alone, it is why the buying power of a single US dollar has decreased over the years, and why wages must increase to match inflation.

This does not mean there has to be mandatory raises to the minimum wage every set number of months or years. Rather Congress should consider the economic environments across our nation, and determine if the minimum wage should be raised every few years. Just as the census every ten years redefines our state's congressional seats, so must a financial report determine whether the minimum wage should be raised to accommodate for inflation

As the minimum wage has been raised many times throughout our history, it is time to raise it again to **$15.00** an hour. The current economic environment is not providing enough jobs paying more than the **$7.25** minimum wage. So until investors and entrepreneurs create more jobs like this, we need to make sure anyone who has to work forty hours a week can still maintain a living.

The choice for **$15** is also not a random number thought of for no reason. It is also not an unrealistic, pie-in-the-sky type dream. As discussed in the previous chapters, the new system will allow businesses to afford this increase in wages for those with employees currently earning less per hour. In today's economic market, this is the minimum amount a single person can finance their life with.

For all those who have looked for apartments to rent across this nation, **$7.25** an hour does not provide enough income to rent most places. In the past month, I myself have just gone through the moving process. In my area of Pennsylvania, the average price for a one-bedroom apartment usually ranged **$800 - $900**. With my current income of **$12.00** per hour, it equates to **$24,960** per year before taxes. Using the current tax rate of **17.45%**, that means my net income is **$20,604** or approximately **$1,717** per month.

While this looks like I can afford any apartment I want in that price range, the decision is not up to me. Several of the apartment complexes in the area I spoke with all had the same requirement, proof of income that is three times the rent. For an apartment that costs **$800** a month, they wanted to see paystubs where my monthly income equated to **$2,400** minimum. In order to make this amount after taxes are taken out is approximately **$16.77** an hour.

Required Monthly Minimum	$2,400	X 12	= $28,800	Minimum Yearly Income Required Post-Tax
		[Compliment of Current Tax Rate]		
Minimum Income Required Post-Tax	$28,800	÷ 0.8255	= $34,888	Minimum Income To Earn Pre Tax
Minimum Income To Earn Pre Tax	$34,888	÷ 52	= 670.92	Weekly Earnings
Weekly Earnings	670.92	÷ 40	= $16.77	Income Needed per Hour

Aside from the fact of how ridiculous a wage expectation that is, this is why so many Americans are struggling in today's society. In my example, I am discussing an apartment at relatively low cost in my area. The national average for the rent of a one-bedroom apartment is **$1,180** according to *apartmentlist.com* as of **May 2016**. Where this gets financially difficult is when you are working two jobs at minimum wage or near, and are trying to support a family.

For arguments sake, let us say these wages are **$9.00** for **30** hours a week, and **$10.50** an hour for **24** hours. The names of the companies are arbitrary, but for millions of Americans, this is the current system they are trying to work with to provide for their families. These jobs include many cashier jobs, and entry level positions at fast food, restaurant, and retail businesses. While these are typically not the jobs Americans want to work as careers, they are the only ones currently available until jobs in industries like manufacturing and construction increase in our nation again.

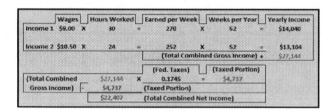

	Wages		Hours Worked		Earned per Week		Weeks per Year		Yearly Income
Income 1	$9.00	X	30	=	270	X	52	=	$14,040
Income 2	$10.50	X	24	=	252	X	52	=	$13,104
					(Total Combined Gross Income)			+	$27,144
				(Fed. Taxes)		(Taxed Portion)			
(Total Combined	$27,144	X	0.1745	=	$4,737				
Gross Income)	-	$4,737	(Taxed Portion)						
		$22,407	(Total Combined Net Income)						

As we can see, someone who currently works **54** hours a week, earning far more than the minimum wage in two jobs, still cannot afford a basic one-bedroom apartment. The saddest truth being this individual works way harder than I only working **40** hours a week, compared to their **54** hours. Due to the ACA as discussed earlier, this is why many Americans are working two jobs as shown.

However, as we can now see, this does not provide the necessary income to survive. Additionally, we are seeing these workers lose out on huge potentials of income. The current regulations from the department of labor demand that once workers go over **40** hours of labor, they be paid time and a half. With two employers this does not apply, meaning despite working that extra **14** hours, you will not receive time and a half pay as would be required from one employer.

Speaking of time and a half, with many employers having to raise the minimum wage to **$15.00** an hour, overtime pay could financially ruin some small businesses. It is important that overtime pay remain a part of the pay structure, but without becoming a burden. To make sure this condition exists, overtime pay can be reduced to time and a quarter pay. Basically that would reduce overtime pay from **$22.50** an hour to **$18.75** at the new minimum wage.

The most common argument against raising the minimum wage, is often stating the workers at these jobs do not deserve this income. Saying that most of these workers at McDonalds or Walmart for example are just high school or college students. They believe these students need to work harder to earn a wage that high. Here is the common misconception though, it may be true that these are school students learning a job and earning income between school. That does not mean these students are working full time.

The other problem as stated, is that these jobs are no longer just employed by students. Many parents are trying to provide for their families on these incomes.

The truth is, it really does not matter what type a job a person is doing. Everyone is worth the same absolute minimum. What I mean by this, is that it is the federal government's responsibility to make sure companies are paying their employees enough to earn a proper living in our nation.

During the sixties and seventies, the minimum wage was almost adjusted on a yearly basis. Due to changes in the economy and inflation, these adjustments are necessary to make sure those on the bottom floor do not end up drowning in poverty as they are now. The time for debate is over, we need to implement a higher minimum wage which in turn will provide economic growth. A higher minimum wage that will in turn provide the service it was meant to provide. A guarantee that if you work forty hours in this country, then you should be able to provide for you and your family.

For those that think this is some lavish wage by the way, remember the following: for a **$15.00** minimum wage, that equates to **$31,200** a year before taxes. After taxes under this new system, that leaves the employee with **$23,400**. This gets us close the target requested by most apartment complexes. So assuming this person rents that one-bedroom apartment costing **$800** a month or **$9,600** a year. This only allows a remaining **$13,800** to afford for other bills and upkeep costs.

The minimum wage is not meant to provide a lavish lifestyle, but be able to provide enough finances for people to take care of themselves. More importantly this is why moving forward, the plan incorporates the minimum wage's FTE value as the same value to determine the amounts given to those who are not in the workforce. Those enrolled in disability, or on social security will receive the same amount through federal direct deposit as if they were employed.

This way when it is time to adjust the minimum wage for cost of living and inflation, it also increases the benefits for the citizens on these programs at the same time. As this plan further shows, simplification of our government is key to success. Meanwhile all sides benefit, citizens benefit from programs designed to help them, and departments like the IRS and DHHS can now function and enforce simplified laws and programs.

With so many changes being done at once, it is understandable to be worried and cautious during what is already an uncertain world. The truth is Americans can wait no longer, which is why these changes must all be written out in one amendment to our constitution. The next chapter will discuss how an amendment can implement these changes, and how certain departments will regulate new programs.

New Regulations

Politicians for years have dodged their duties to protect the wellbeing of their citizenry. This election has brought to the forefront every major problem that must be addressed now if our nation is to avoid the way of Rome. We cannot continue living on the verge of economic collapse every four or eight years. We cannot continue living in a society that taxes its citizens without actual representation.

As a recap, the first change was the tax structure. That becomes simplified by removing every page in our current tax code, and hitting the reset button. By using the resources Congress already has authority to raise revenue by, a balanced budget can be made. In order to maintain the welfare of the people as the constitution states it protects, the new amendment will permanently add the Single-Payer Health Insurance Program, Social Security, and Disability as constitutional rights to our citizens.

Furthermore, a minimum wage will now also be required to be set by Congress. The minimum wage will be applied to all workers in the United States, and incomes will now be taxed fairly based on the framework proposed earlier. Social Security and Disability benefits will no longer be calculated by convoluted equations, and replaced with the *Full Time Equivalent* amount set by the minimum wage. With this amendment that will start at **$15.00** an hour, or the FTE of **$31,200**.

The final source of revenue will come from a uniform excise tax system on certain products approved by Congress. For purposes to maintain a balanced budget, the framework proposed in the earlier section is strongly suggested to be implemented with everything else. The most important being the excise tax on all stock trades. This means capital gains would no longer be classified as income under the income tax as it would then be unjustly taxed twice.

That is the tradeoff, capital gains are no longer classified as income while the service to trade stocks are taxed. Since stock markets are gambling with investor's money, why should this service not be taxed? Many crimes have been committed by the financial sectors and political sectors of our nation. It is time to end the corruption and begin a process that will benefit everyone.

As shown earlier, even just collecting five cents on every dollar traded on that market could equate to around **$3.150** trillion. This alone funds **74%** of the *Department of Health and Human Services'* budget, which I estimated earlier at **$4.235** trillion. While I know investors will be worried about this tax hurting investments, the truth is your getting a better deal to earn just as much money if not more in the market. Think about it, would you rather be taxed **5%** both ways on your stock investment, or pay the potential **50%** income tax if that capital gain is in or puts you in that income tax bracket? In most cases, that **5%** is going to hurt you far less than the income tax percentage.

As discussed earlier was also the taxation on recreational marijuana products. It is time to undo the damages caused by marijuana being a schedule one controlled substance under *The Controlled Substance Act*. This legislation has been a mistake and an overstep in constitutional authority as done prior in the prohibition of alcohol. Prohibition and manufacture of sale during the early **1900's** led to disaster. With higher crime rates and gang wars occurring, violence was increasing while a profitable economy was shoved underground.

The same thing has happened with marijuana. The majority of public opinion now favors legal use at **58%** according to a *Gallup* poll on **October 21ˢᵗ 2015**. It is time to allow this economy to rise aboveground, and let the states regulate it how they see fit. Then for those states and territories that legalize recreational use, now they have a whole new industry that's providing jobs and wealth in their states and localities.

That is what bring us to the next part of the amendment. With the introduction of a single-payer health insurance program, the regulation of all drugs and medications will need to be re-grouped and organized by the FDA. Then the DHHS will write a drug formulary for all medical providers and pharmacies to follow in terms of reimbursement. The states will then have the final say to allow what products are allowed in their territories.

In terms of marijuana, that means the states and territories have the option to legalize both, one, or none of the purposes for marijuana. This power, and the power to tax businesses needs to be returned to the states. This is why state governments also receive a good deal here. Once again states can have the final say as to what is and is not allowed in their territory. Secondly, with the federal government removing all taxes on businesses, the states and local governments can now tax those businesses appropriately to compete for their jobs and income that they provide.

The only federal regulations regarding businesses, in addition to all environmental and work safety regulations, is that they pay all their employees a minimum wage of **$15.00** an hour. As discussed in this section, the removal of FICA taxes and ACA regulations are going to allow existing businesses and new ones to prosper and expand. There is one more way this amendment will set up a program to reduce one final cost shared by every business.

This expense is the hiring expense that can vary greatly from month to month, from business to business. As an employer, looking for new employees to fill gaps in coverage is often a burden financially. Between loss of income from low productivity, and any cost associated with job posting and interviewing is a drain on business income.

How this is fixed is a program run by the *Department of Labor*. With all these changes to our economy, we will need a system in place to help relocate jobs for all those that become unemployed for when existing health insurance companies cease operations. Basically, the government would oversee a system similar to that of a temp agency. The difference would be that instead of this service charging the business for use, or garnishing wages of employees using this service, the service is free for both.

For those who are familiar with *House of Cards*, this may sound similar to Frank Underwood's plan called America Works or *AmWorks*. It is similar cause the idea is based off the show. Even though this is an idea from a show, it does not make it a terrible idea. Millions of people are going to be unemployed. This would become a huge problem for every state budget that offers an unemployment plan.

A problem I have with someone filing for unemployment is when there are usually several jobs down the road that are available. Only if there are no jobs available should someone be able to file for unemployment. It is not fair to those who remain in the workforce to pay for others to sit at home. That is why the responsibility of governments at all levels need to help assist in ensuring everyone can earn their own living.

This is also the point of raising the minimum wage to a living wage. For arguments sake, let us say someone who has worked as an accounted had lost their job due to the company is currently downsizing. Even though their job currently makes more than the minimum wage, they could still theoretically work at a McDonalds and pays their bills as long as they are still working forty hours a week.

The reason why most Americans would not do this is for several reasons. The first is that it looks bad on your résumé. An employer that wants to hire a new accountant will typically want that candidates last job to be in accounting. The problem with this in reality though is that when you lose your job, there may not be an opening of the same exact job available. In which case it is asinine to then just let them leave the workforce to collect unemployment until a job opens up in their profession.

If they choose to remain out of the workforce, then that is fine. The point is no government should be paying for a healthy individual to sit at home. Unless they are on permeant disability, or temporary disability such as worker's compensation, then yes they shall receive benefits that are equal to the current set FTE salary. Otherwise, if they lose their job, then if they want to pay their bills, they need to secure a new job.

Another reason for those often choosing to remain out of the work force is because a change in jobs usually meant trying to find a job that offered greater or equal health benefits. Now with health insurance being run by one government program, employees can focus on gaining an education to work the career of their choice. During periods where their jobs of choice are not available, people can still find employment, and will no longer have to worry about health benefits.

With this being a government run program, a website or local office could list all jobs currently available in the area. This would include all private sector jobs, and all government opportunities. This way all those who are looking for jobs can find something in order to pay their bills. With all jobs at minimum paying **$15.00** an hour, this means any job will now allow a person to stay above poverty. The point being if you want to do more in life, than you still need a college education for a better paying job.

Thus once these programs or websites are operational, all those who were working at health insurance companies or temp agencies which will probably be put out of business by these programs, can find a job to remain employed if they cannot find anything through a traditional source in decent time. There will be those that say it is not the governments job to make sure the populace stays employed. Probably stating the many private companies that provide this service already.

As stated though, private companies charge business to recommend employees to them, and often the employees then have their wages garnished by these companies. Once more states begin to legalize recreational marijuana, that could lead to the potential of thousands of jobs. In addition, this nation's infrastructure is crumbling, and thus thousand more jobs will be needed to be filled that way as well. By having a government service which shows job searchers potential employers, it expedites the unemployment process.

Considering a larger portion of federal income is connected to the amount of income earned by our populace, it is imperative that we focus a portion of effort on pursuing **100%** employment. As stated there are approximately **8.297** million people without jobs. Once employed that can equate to an increase of **$64.717** billion dollars in federal revenue. More importantly, with an increase in people employed and earning enough money to live a respectable life, there will be an overall increase in the standard of living in the US. We can start to see the middle class return to our nation as opposed to its current disappearing act.

A program like this run by the DOL will also help many seasonal and agricultural jobs. These employers often have trouble finding employees for these positions. As stated earlier though, every job will now need to pay **$15.00** an hour, therefore if anyone is between work, every job at full time hours will provide a fair income to maintain a living. Therefore, if nothing else is available, then any citizen or immigrant looking for work can find something part time till other jobs open up.

While many argue that immigrants are stealing American jobs, these people are also often bigoted. The sad truth is many Americans would rather be collecting unemployment than earn a decent living. As long as we have a system that encourages unemployment over working, that will remain the case. Once this program is up a running, there will no longer be a reason for the federal or state governments wasting tax dollars for those on unemployment. As long as there is a help wanted sign in a McDonalds, there is a job that someone can provide for themselves working forty hours a week.

The cost for a program like this would not be much. It can be started at **$56** billion dollars, **$1** billion to set up a minimum of one office in each state and territory. It would be best to start with the areas with highest unemployment, and areas that need major infrastructure projects. Since state governments will no longer have to provide any funds for health insurance, it could be encouraged for them to allocate those funds in these job programs or increase the amount spent on education.

The last section deals with the final three changes that need to be addressed to fix our nation, and return the democracy to our populace. The truth is our nation did not get to the sad state it is currently in by accident. Our current situation is by design of the establishment and financial oligarchy that is currently in control of the United States.

This is discussed further, but there are two things that must be done to reverse the damage done. The first is that campaign finance reform must occur to remove the grasp money currently has on politics. Once removed by eliminating super PACs, we can also change the process of elections. The current political parties hold too much control of our federal election process. It is time to return our nation to a democracy and allow us to vote for our representatives again.

The final change is a change discussed earlier. In order for the health insurance program to work, it requires a new card system for all citizens and legal residents. While this is done, we can finally settle a problem that has caused issues for decades. Many illegal residents came here on a flawed visa system which has now timed out, or crossed the southern border looking for better opportunity and freedom. It is time to create a system that brings everyone out from the shadows, and ensure a fair system for future immigrants.

Campaign Finance & Election Reform

Since the disastrous decision of Citizen's United, the money has poured into the election process as if it were a newly opened casino. The decision has further legalized what was once considered bribery. The effort continues to get money out of politics, but has been difficult considering those who make the rules, do not want it to change. It has been this corruption that has caused government policy to favor corporate interests for decades.

While discussing change, it is time to discuss the final changes to be implemented in the next amendment. In addition to a balanced budget and better welfare programs, it is time to change how presidential elections work. These changes include finally limiting money in federal elections and how debates shall be structured. No longer will establishment figures, and corporations with their media puppets tell us who are acceptable government officials.

Despite America being considered a democracy, this election year in particular has shown us another story. The content of this story range from voter suppression, to absolute chaos in many of the primaries and caucuses this year. If a nation is going to promote democracy, they must also know what it truly means to be democratic. Moving forward, it is time one person finally had one vote, and give the government back to *We the People*, the rightful owners.

Campaign Finance Laws

Every election cycle, the media begins to report how more money will be spent in the election. While it is of course necessary for campaigns to raise money to pay for campaign costs, it was intended this money come from individuals. Individuals that are donating to a candidate because they believe in the message and policies of the political candidate. The creation of super PAC's has instead allowed for the wealthy to buy politicians to do their bidding.

While the Citizens United decision is the most recent case of undermining contribution laws, it is not how this all started. Originally, our government tried to limit money in politics as done by the *Tillman Act* of **1907**. This was the first piece of legislation designed to prohibit corporate contributions to political campaigns. Without the *Federal Election Commission* (FEC) though, there was no one to enforce this law.

In **1971**, Congress passed the *Federal Election Campaign Act* (FECA), which became the foundation for regulating all political contributions. This included regulating funds, and increased disclosure of those contributions. In **1974**, the act was amended which placed limits on donations, and created the FEC to enforce these laws.

It was not until **1976**, that the courts at the time began creating the problems in campaign finance we have today. In the case *Buckley v. Valeo*, the Supreme Court struck down several parts of the **1974** amendments to FECA. The most important part of this decision was the ruling that limitations on funds spent by campaigns and individuals were unconstitutional. This decision now equates spending money to a form of speech protected under the first amendment.

That alone did not cause problems, and in fact the court upheld the section that limited the amount of money donated to campaigns. The problem occurs from the precedent this case made determining that spending money equates to free speech. The real issues began two years later in **1978** after the case *First National Bank of Boston v. Bellotti*. The Supreme Court ruled corporations are protected by the first amendment of the constitution. In short, the court in *Buckley v. Valeo* stated money equates to speech, and then two years later said corporations have freedom of speech.

It is these two decisions in which influenced the ruling of *Citizens United*. While it is natural for any court to follow previous judicial precedents, the problem is that this precedent has removed our democracy from us. In the second presidential election since the decision, millionaires and billionaires have been throwing money at candidates trying to buy the election. According to *opensecrets.org*, currently **2,305** super PACs have raised a combined **$754,308,666** as of **June 10ᵗʰ 2016**. While it is ridiculous how much money is spent on elections, it is also funny to point out the millions of dollars wasted on failed presidential candidates like Jeb Bush for example. During his presidential run in the republican primary, super PACs supporting him wasted a combined **$104,124,340**.

While it is somewhat a sigh of relief that millionaires and billionaires cannot just out right buy the presidency, it is troublesome however that this is still legal. Presidential candidates are supposed to be citizens who are volunteering for the job to lead the country and help all Americans. A leader that is dedicated to all, not just private interests that bankroll them and their political party's ideology.

Many running for public office in favor of super PACs will argue that more money in politics is a good thing. That this increase of speech is good for the public to increase information. Of course what they are not discussing is how they are working for the wealthiest donors that back them. While the regulations of super PACs state that there is to be no communication between the candidates and the PACs backing them, we all know that this is not being enforced. How could it be?

Besides the foolishness of relying on people to use the honor system in politics, super PACs have allowed for legal bribery. It is not called bribery, because that would be illegal then. What then do you name our current political environment? An environment in which politicians spend most of their time pandering to millionaires and billionaires at dinner events and fundraisers. Some of these events range in cost from as little as **$10,000** a dinner plate, to as much as hundreds of thousands of dollars. It is naïve to not believe private discussions are happening between donors and candidates about topics ranging from votes on bills, to how super PAC money can and should be spent.

This is the exact definition of bribery. Politicians are receiving money in return for favors, plain and simple. Before, politicians would listen to the problems of Americans and solve them. The reason being those politicians understood that to earn the votes of their constitutes, they had to listen to the problems affecting them, and come up with solutions. With super PACs raising millions of dollars, politicians no longer care for your problems, or even their own ideology and beliefs.

Politicians have become sell outs to support a system that will finance their political careers as long as they are willing to play ball. It is the reason why you see all these millions of dollars to finance these campaigns. Rich people are not just making these donations out of the kindness of their heart. These are business people, meaning that any time they spend a large sum of money, they are looking for a return on investment.

It is why we will see corporations donate to the same politicians, super PACs that support them, and the political parties in general at times. With a system so focused on greed, it is the reason for gridlock in congress, and why no significant legislation has passed to fix the problems like income inequality and tax reform. Since the current system is why many of these rich and elite are as wealthy as they are, they do not want it to change. They are paying max dollar to politicians to insure the system remains to favor them.

With a congress bought out by the rich, we need an amendment to fix these problems. A constitutional convention called by the State legislatures can bypass the corruption in Washington. Once money is no longer the primary objective of a politician's campaign, we can focus on the issues again and move forward. Of course as stated earlier, if we are proposing an amendment, we might as well fix as many problems as quickly as possible.

So then what is the fix to our current campaign finanace laws? The first nonnegotiable aspect is that super PACs must come to an end. The second is we need to revision how not only money is used in our system, but also how the federal election process as a whole operates. Before we discuss the potentials of that, let us first look at the current limits on campaign contributions.

Image From: *http://www.fec.gov/pages/brochures/contrib.shtml*

CONTRIBUTION LIMITS FOR 2015-2016 FEDERAL ELECTIONS

DONORS	RECIPIENTS				
	Candidate Committee	PAC[1] (SSF and Nonconnected)	State/District/Local Party Committee	National Party Committee	Additional National Party Committee Accounts[2]
Individual	$2,700* per election	$5,000 per year	$10,000 per year (combined)	$33,400* per year	$100,200* per account, per year
Candidate Committee	$2,000 per election	$5,000 per year	Unlimited Transfers	Unlimited Transfers	
PAC – Multicandidate	$5,000 per election	$5,000 per year	$5,000 per year (combined)	$15,000 per year	$45,000 per account, per year
PAC – Nonmulticandidate	$2,700* per election	$5,000 per year	$10,000 per year (combined)	$33,400* per year	$100,200* per account, per year
State, District & Local Party Committee	$5,000 per election	$5,000 per year	Unlimited Transfers		
National Party Committee	$5,000 per election[3]	$5,000 per year			

* Indexed for inflation in odd-numbered years.

1. "PAC" here refers to a committee that makes contributions to other federal political committees. Independent-expenditure-only political committees (sometimes called "super PACs") may accept unlimited contributions, including from corporations and labor organizations.

2. The limits in this column apply to a national party committee's accounts for: (i) the presidential nominating convention; (ii) election recounts and contests and other legal proceedings; and (iii) national party headquarters buildings. A party's national committee, Senate campaign committee and House campaign committee are each considered separate national party committees with separate limits. Only a national party committee, not the parties' national congressional campaign committees, may have an account for the presidential nominating convention.

3. Additionally, a national party committee and its Senatorial campaign committee may contribute up to $46,800 combined per campaign to each Senate candidate.

The chart is from the FEC's website and once again shows the commonality in our policies. Another complicated system in which multiple parties and entities are involved. This chart also shows another part of the corruption and unaccountable money in our system. That is all the rules and regulations on donations to political parties. It is the fact that these large sums of money can be donated to political parties, which is why you hear the political fundraisers that take place. A portion goes to the candidate, and the rest to the party.

This is the reason why politicians only address the issues of their wealthiest donors. This is because not only their personal campaigns rely on it, but politicians are also strong-armed to play ball with these donors to benefit their political parties as a whole. This is why the primary race this election cycle has been so important.

While many Americans knew of this system taking place as politics as usual, they were ok with it or went along with it because they were part of the middle class.

The year is **2016** now, and the middle class is near extinction. Americans are no longer ignoring the smokescreens created by the political and financial elites in our nation. The truth is our current nation is more in line with an *oligarchy*. By definition it is a country that is run by the wealthy and elites. Those in power of our nation is the clear struggle between the major political parties in America, the *Republicans* and *Democrats*. However, behind the scenes are the wealthy donors and elites financing individual campaigns in elections, and the corporate owned media reporting on these elections.

This is also not a new conclusion. Back in **2014** there was a joint study by Princeton and Northwestern universities about policies enacted by congress between **1981** and **2002**. Before stating their findings, it is important to remember that **1981** was three years after the court decision saying corporations have free speech and thus allowed to donate unlimited amounts of money for political purposes. After looking at **1,779** different policy issues at this time, they wrote, *"our analyses suggest that majorities of the American public actually have little influence over the policies our government adopts"*.

So the question at hand, how should our federal election processes work? If America is to be a democracy again, policy needs to be influenced by all Americans, not the wealthy donors and elite. How this can be accomplished is by removing the corrupt financing system currently in place, and regulated by the FEC. The FEC should be regulating donations to political candidates like the IRS regulates income of all citizens.

My proposal will remove the systemic corruption in our system and allow for all citizens to be heard again. Lastly the vast amounts of power the current political parties in our nation enjoy must come to an end. They have created a system that has divided the nation. Now you are either a republican or democrat. No longer is there allowed middle ground to discuss issues. Despite the system of political absolutes our government operates in, **42%** of Americans identify as independents according to a *Gallup* article from **January 11ᵗʰ 2016**.

In the next chapter I will discuss more how we need to remove power from our political parties. For a fair election process to take place, all contributions should only be made by individuals. After all, people, not corporations, are the ones who vote for candidates in elections. This change in policy will also reduce the workload for the FEC to keep track of every donation. We can finally implement a system where one person will have one vote, and one voice.

What I mean by one voice is that in the current system, sure we can all donate the maximum amount of **$2,700** to the political candidate we like, and if we were wealthy maybe donate the max amounts to political parties. However not all Americans can then donate millions of dollars to super PACs, or have businesses, shell LLCs, or charity organizations to donate millions more. Below should be the new chart used by the FEC to regulate all federal election campaign donations.

Federal Election Positions	Congress: House of Representatives	Congress: Senate	Presidency
Individual Contrabution Amounts to be Reported by Social Security Number	$2,000	$3,000	$5,000

As our constitution sets up, there are three federal positions that all American citizens can vote for. Thereby it makes sense that only citizens can provide money for the candidates they believe in, in each election. Ever since corporations were given the protection of first amendment rights, they have spent billions of dollars over the years influencing elections.

Money spent creating a system that favors them and the political elites, screws over the average worker. Billions of dollars that should have been used to pay workers higher wages over these last decades, have instead gone to buying politicians, and lobbying Congress. Seeing as how this system removes corporations and political parties from the financial system of federal elections all together, it will be no surprise that they will not support a change like this.

As the chart shows, the amount allowed to be donated increases with the office the candidate is running for. All political contributions must now be done by individual citizens. It must be written that all contributions must be recorded with name and social security number. This way when candidates report contributions to the FEC, they can total up donations done by the same person, now verifiable by their social security number.

To be clear though, I am not saying that if corporations or the wealthy want to support a candidate that they cannot. They just can no longer be able to spend millions of dollars on candidates and political establishments like they currently do through shady organizations. If a business owner agrees with the ideology of a political candidate, then they should not be denied to their right to verbally support the candidate. They could spread the message of candidates they agree with or host political events for them. If corporations and businesses want to support a candidate, then just be transparent about it. The difference is those corporations can no longer donate large sums of money to completely buy the loyalty and cooperation of politicians.

For a fair election, everyone's voice should have the ability to be heard at the same volume. It is why for real change to happen; it must come in the form of a constitutional amendment that is demanded by the people. By removing the financial corruption in Washington, our politicians can listen to their constitutes again, and begin solving problems. No longer will there be gridlock, and a polar system controlled by two parties.

New Federal Election Process & Procedures

The political parties of **21st** century America have too much wealth and power. As discussed in the previous chapter, politicians and the elite have spent the past forty years to create a system in which the established and powerful maintain their status. The primary process for the **2016** presidential election has allowed for the many systemic problems in our election process to come to light.

The FEC needs to be responsible for all aspects of the election process in federal elections. Time after time again, we are seeing state primaries be a mockery of the democratic world. Caucuses in Iowa that are called by coin flips to decide a presidential nominee is an absolute disgrace to democracy, let alone the other cases of voter suppression throughout the election.

Before going further, for those who did not make the connection based on my political ideologies earlier, I am a Bernie Sanders supporter. I say this because I understand many people will suggest I am proposing a system to benefit him, or that I am trying to influence the election. My proposal is a system to benefit all Americans in upcoming elections. In terms of this election cycle, the current rules we have are the rules we have to work with.

Senator Sanders has stated this many times throughout the process. The truth is though his campaign has fought an uphill battle with the establishment that already named Hillary Clinton as the Democratic nominee before the primary even took place. The facts are yes, she is leading in pledged delegates, those earned through democratic primaries and caucuses, finishing at **2,219** to Sanders' **1,832**. To current Democratic rules, neither candidate has reached the **2,383** delegates to claim the nomination before the convention starting **July 25th 2016** in Philadelphia, Pennsylvania. It is only at the convention the final **712** *superdelegates* will cast their votes.

One problem during the Democratic primary has been the mainstream media's reporting on superdelegates. In articles, interviews, and images discussing the delegate math, most have included the superdelegates as if they have already voted. This is journalistic malpractice considering that they have not voted yet, and are thus not facts.

By including these delegates as voted in the totals, it can create an illusion of a lead for a candidate. This is the exact scenario created for Hillary Clinton during the **2016** primary. Clinton apparently had a massive lead of **1,234** delegates to **579** delegates for Senator Sanders as reported by the *Wall Street Journal* on **March 15, 2016**. For the voters heading to the polls that day and see this or similar headlines, they think Clinton is already leading by double the number of delegates as Sanders.

In truth, Clinton's lead at this time in pledged delegates was only **761** to Sander's **554**. This is because they had included **473** *superdelegates* in the count for Clinton. The problem is these delegates still have not voted at the time of this article, and do not vote until the *Democratic Convention* at the end of July. This is just one example of the many cases of unfair treatment by the establishment media to Bernie Sanders. Since the beginning of Sanders' campaign, the media did not discuss him or his policies, or when they did mention him, it was often brief calling him a socialist.

It all goes back to the corruption and money in politics. At the beginning of this campaign over a year ago now, no one on the Democratic side wanted to run against Hillary Clinton in the primary. She had all the backing of the establishment, the media, and wealthy donors giving large sums of money into her super PACs. It was at this time the Republican circus was getting ready to come to town, and Clinton did not expect to have to earn the Democratic nomination.

That all changed when one man decided to finally stand up to the corruption in Washington. Senator Sanders has a message in his campaign for president. That message is removing the corruption that money in politics has created, and provide a better future for all Americans. The problem for the establishment is they like money in politics.

Now that someone is standing up and saying they will change the system, we have seen a primary in which the entire corrupt system has fought back against that candidate. The debate schedule is another example of how the *Democratic National Committee* (DNC) tried to limit the public's exposure to Sanders' message. Before the first votes were cast on **February 1st** in Iowa this year, the DNC hosted only four debates and one town hall style event. Two of these debates were on Saturday nights, which as could be expected had low views, as compared to the *seven* debates done by the Republicans, all on weeknights.

In addition to the poor debate schedule, for those who remember turning on any news network during this time, the majority of coverage was on something bigoted that Donald Trump said. That in fact has been the cycle of the **2016** primary, Trump says something racist, sexist, xenophobic, or some other ignorant comment, and then that's all the media talked about. Then the irony is they wonder how Trump became the Republican nominee. Over the course of this election, Trump had received a little under **$2** billion in free media according to *The New York Times* in an article from **March 15ᵗʰ 2016**. This is more than double the amount Clinton received in second.

So with that being the stage set for this election cycle's primary, let us now look at the results of the two major parties. The next page shows the breakdown of each states primary result as of **June 16ᵗʰ 2016**.

Voting Populace: Calculated by taking each of the states estimated population, and subtracting those under 18.

Popular Vote Totals: Recorded from *Google* searches which reported totals from the *Associated Press* as of 6/16/2016

Remaining Voters: Calculated by subtracting all reported votes from the total *Voting Populace* estimates.

State Primaries	Open / Closed	Date (D)	Date (R)	Voting Populace	Clinton	Sanders	Cruz	Kasich	Rubio	Trump	Remaing Voters	Voter Turnout
Iowa	Hybrid	1-Feb		2,223,497	701	697	51,666	3,474	43,165	45,427	2,078,367	6.53%
New Hampshire	Hybrid	9-Feb		990,135	95,252	151,584	33,189	44,909	30,032	100,606	534,763	45.99%
Nevada	Closed	20-Feb	23-Feb	2,000,646	6,316	5,678	16,079	2,709	17,940	34,531	1,917,393	4.16%
South Carolina	Hybrid	27-Feb	20-Feb	3,409,507	271,514	95,977	164,790	56,206	165,881	239,851	2,415,288	29.16%
Colorado	Hybrid	1-Mar	9-Apr	3,691,221	49,314	72,115	0		0		3,569,792	3.29%
Arkansas	Open			2,128,496	144,580	64,868	123,873	15,094	101,235	133,144	1,545,698	27.38%
Alabama	Open			3,534,452	309,928	76,399	180,608	37,970	159,802	371,735	2,398,010	32.15%
Georgia	Open			6,950,624	543,008	214,332	505,109	72,303	315,979	501,707	4,998,186	28.09%
Massachusetts	Hybrid			4,896,559	603,784	586,716	60,473	113,783	112,822	311,313	3,107,668	36.53%
Minnesota	Open	1-Mar		3,889,227	73,510	118,135	32,684	6,488	41,126	24,018	3,593,266	7.61%
Oklahoma	Hybrid			2,712,593	139,338	174,054	157,941	16,515	119,562	130,141	1,975,042	27.19%
Tenessee	Hybrid			4,700,466	245,304	120,333	211,159	65,243	180,989	332,702	3,564,736	24.16%
Texas	Hybrid			17,715,605	935,080	475,561	1,239,370	120,257	502,223	757,618	13,685,496	22.75%
Vermont	Open			471,768	18,335	115,863	5,929	18,543	11,778	19,868	281,352	40.36%
Virginia	Hybrid			5,912,985	503,358	275,507	173,193	96,519	327,042	355,960	4,181,406	29.28%
Kansas	Closed	5-Mar		2,049,278	12,593	26,450	35,207	7,795	12,189	35,207	1,919,837	6.32%
Louisiana	Top-Two			3,290,774	221,615	72,240	113,949	19,355	33,804	124,818	2,704,993	17.80%
Nebraska	Top-Two	5-Mar	10-May	1,318,079	14,340	19,120	36,418	22,526	0	121,287	1,104,388	16.21%
Maine	Closed	6-Mar	5-Mar	1,019,594	1,232	2,231	8,550	2,270	1,492	6,070	997,749	2.14%
Michigan	Open	8-Mar		7,317,362	576,795	595,222	330,015	321,655	123,673	483,751	4,886,251	33.22%
Mississippi	Hybrid			2,123,241	182,447	36,348	147,065	35,817	20,768	191,795	1,509,041	28.93%
Florida	Closed	15-Mar		14,391,694	1,097,400	566,603	403,640	159,412	636,653	1,077,221	10,450,765	27.38%
Illinois	Hybrid			9,408,056	1,017,006	982,017	434,038	282,874	124,568	556,916	6,010,637	36.11%
Missouri	Open			4,395,560	310,602	309,071	380,367	92,553	57,006	382,093	2,863,888	34.85%
North Carolina	Hybrid			7,002,737	616,383	460,316	418,740	144,299	87,858	458,151	4,816,990	31.21%
Ohio	Hybrid			8,506,569	679,266	513,549	267,592	956,762	59,418	727,585	5,302,397	37.67%
Arizona	Hybrid	22-Mar		4,628,522	235,697	163,400	132,147	53,040	0	249,916	3,794,322	18.02%
Utah	Hybrid			1,850,474	15,666	61,333	122,567	29,773	0	24,864	1,596,271	13.74%
Idaho	Hybrid	22-Mar	8-Mar	1,110,755	5,065	18,640	100,942	16,517	35,347	62,478	871,766	21.52%
Alaska	Hybrid	26-Mar	1-Mar	497,727	99	440	7,973	892	3,318	7,346	477,659	4.03%
Hawaii	Open	26-Mar	8-Mar	1,016,159	10,125	23,530	4,379	1,413	1,759	5,677	969,276	4.61%
Washington	Top-Two	26-Mar	24-May	5,008,436	7,140	19,159	55,719	52,129	0	481,089	4,471,286	10.72%
Wisconsin	Open	5-Apr		4,201,091	432,767	567,936	531,129	155,200	0	386,371	2,127,689	49.35%
Wyoming	Closed	9-Apr	16-Apr	415,137	124	156	644	0	189	70	413,954	0.28%
New York	Closed	19-Apr		14,493,452	1,054,083	763,469	126,151	217,904	0	524,932	11,806,913	18.54%
Connecticut	Hybrid			2,641,476	170,075	152,410	24,969	68,481	0	123,307	2,110,174	20.11%
Delaware	Closed			668,525	55,950	36,659	11,110	14,225	0	42,472	508,109	24.00%
Maryland	Hybrid	26-Apr		4,286,123	533,247	281,275	19,792	100,089	0	236,673	3,052,851	28.77%
Pennsylvania	Closed			9,498,330	918,689	719,955	340,201	304,793	0	892,702	6,321,990	33.44%
Rhode Island	Hybrid			786,760	52,493	66,720	6,393	14,929	0	39,659	607,166	22.83%
Indiana	Hybrid	3-May		4,694,121	303,382	335,256	406,280	83,913	0	590,460	2,974,830	36.63%
West Virginia	Hybrid	10-May		1,417,695	86,354	123,860	18,208	11,685	0	156,245	1,019,343	28.10%
Kentucky	Closed	17-May	5-Mar	3,193,812	212,550	210,626	72,503	33,134	37,579	32,481	2,544,927	20.32%
Oregon	Hybrid	17-May		2,881,834	251,739	320,746	61,590	59,096	0	241,804	1,947,859	32.41%
California	Top-Two			27,170,431	1,940,580	1,502,043	144,125	176,628	0	1,174,829	22,232,234	18.17%
Montana	Open	7-Jun		739,858	55,194	63,168	14,474	10,622	0	114,056	482,342	34.81%
New Jersey	Closed			6,544,590	554,237	323,259	27,521	59,506	0	356,697	5,223,370	20.19%
New Mexico	Closed			1,499,956	110,451	103,856	13,825	7,870	0	71,530	1,190,424	20.64%
South Dakota	Hybrid			581,102	27,046	25,958	11,352	10,659	0	44,666	461,221	20.63%
North Dakota	Open	7-Jun	1-Apr	498,347	101	253	0	0	0		497,993	0.01%
District of Columbia	Closed	14-Jun	12-Mar	461,896	75,223	20,137	351	1,009	1,059	391	363,726	21.25%
Totals:				226,837,334	15,777,078	12,035,230	7,648,237	4,172,814	3,366,256	13,356,655	170,481,094	24.84%
Percent of Vote:					6.96%	5.31%	3.37%	1.84%	1.48%	5.88%		75.16%

Two things to note about the following chart. The first being the voting populace is just an estimate. They were calculated by using the estimates in each state and subtracting all people under **18**. Therefore, these voter populace estimates might be higher than actual counts since it does not take into account if any of those in each state were legal residents, or how many prisoners are in each state.

Even though both parties use a delegate system in their primaries, the popular vote shows a much better picture of what the country is thinking. There are many flaws that should be addressed to provide fair elections moving forward. The first being the fact that all states do not vote at the same time. What makes this more annoying is the fact that some states will vote on two different days depending on the individual party. Politics can be confusing enough for people, let alone having a system that is far more complicated than necessary. Depending on party affiliation, you may or may not be able to vote in that day's primary.

Where this becomes a major issue is that those voting first always have way less information than those voting at the end. Unless citizens were paying full attention to politics from the summer of **2015** till the date of their primary, chances are, those voting early in the process are in fact very uneducated about the candidates running. This is by no fault of the citizens, but our entire political culture. Instead of the media reporting on candidates' positions and their solutions, way too often they are only reporting on some meaningless five second sound bite or twitter comment.

How theses contests operate also differ from state to state depending on party. Primaries are relatively straight forward in that there is a list of candidates, and then those in that state vote on them. The delegates are awarded based on the system agreed on by each individual party. This gets complicated in two ways. The first is that not all primary contests are simple votes. Several states go through a voting process called a *Caucus*. This process usually involves multiple hours of time from the voters, in which they will discuss the candidates, and then vote on delegates to vote in another voting process.

One such example of the havoc these caucuses create was that in the Nevada Caucus for the Democrats. From the initial vote, Clinton did win, but only **13** out of the total **23** delegates that are considered *district-level*. These delegates are awarded proportionally based on the popular vote. Nevada offers **43** total delegates, **8** that are superdelegates, which do not vote till the national convention, and an additional **12** delegates that are not awarded until the state's party convention.

After the initial vote, there are two more stages of voting. On **April 2ed**, there were county conventions which is where the debacle begins. At this stage in the process, delegates who were elected in the initial vote, now have to show up again to vote on the delegates to go to the state convention. The reason this became a debacle is because since Clinton won the initial vote, it was expected she was to have more delegates show up at the county conventions.

However, **2,124** delegates showed up for Sanders as opposed to only **1,722** for Clinton. This now meant going into the state convention, Sanders would have **55%** of the delegates on his side to Clinton's **45%** to determine the final **12** delegates. After this surprise, many thought then that Sanders would have more delegates going into the state convention, thus possibly come out with at least less of a gap if not more delegates then Clinton in the state overall.

This of course is not how the state convention on **May 14ᵗʰ** proceeded. At the start of the convention, the rules committee had denied **64** Sanders delegates entry stating they were not registered Democrats or some similar paperwork issue. While **8** Clinton delegates were also denied access for similar reasons, this ended up giving Clinton a **31** delegate advantage in the convention. After a convention in which the Chairwomen Roberta Lange ignores the voice votes and denies a request for a recount, Clinton ends up with **20** delegates to Sanders' **15** for the national convention.

This was the original breakdown of delegates had the DNC just used the primary vote to allocate all delegates originally. What makes it hilarious is by their flawed system, Sander's almost walked away with more delegates despite losing the initial vote. The truth of the corruption of those in power though is greatly shown through the state convention, and in many other instances of voter suppression throughout the nation. While those in the DNC could have just allowed this process to take place and let the votes happen, instead they step in and remove delegates from Sanders to improve their odds. To secure about **3** delegates for Clinton, they infuriate every Sanders supporter across the nation.

Now this was only one state for only one party. Every other state has its own process usually simpler than the one just described. On the other hand, in some of the Republican primaries, they did not even have a popular vote. That is why under Colorado and North Dakota, no one voted for republicans because there was no primary. For us to be considered a democracy, this whole process is a disgrace.

With a system as complicated as this, this is why only about **25%** of the electorate comes out to vote in primaries. This systematic removal from the voting process is why people feel disenfranchised from their government. The other reason why turnout is low because many Americans cannot vote in the primary at all. For the states with closed primaries, you must be a voter registered with a political party, and can only vote in that party's election. This is the reason why our nation is so polarized as it is because a system like this encourages it. When you are only allowed to vote for the party you are a member of, you begin to care less about the issues and more about your party retaining power.

Voters registered as Republicans or Democrats are at their lowest in Gallup's polling history. With **42%** identifying as independents, that is approximately **95,271,680** voters who do not care about the policies of Republicans or Democrats. What independents care about is what all voters should care about. That is what are the polices of the individual candidate, and not their party affiliation. As it happens most polls continually show a larger amount of independents agree with the policies of Bernie Sanders than the other candidates.

This is the frustration many independents and Sanders supporters alike have with the current system besides its corruption. The establishment has been wanting Sanders to drop out so they can *unite* the party for the general election. The truth is, the majority of the **12** million people that voted for Sanders was not because he was a democrat. We voted for him because he has ideas and a plan to move this country forward. When looking at results of the primary, it is important to notice which states have open primaries, and which ones are closed.

The reason being is because as stated, there are millions of votes that were not taken in the primary. In a general election, we finally have the freedom to vote for whoever we want. As the DNC readies for its convention this July, the superdelegates have one question to ask themselves before they vote. *Which candidate presents a more winnable candidacy against the Republicans in November?*

Yes, it is true Hillary Clinton earned **3** million more votes in the popular count, and more pledged delegates. However, both candidates did not reach the number needed outright for the nomination, so superdelegates need to really think about that question. While those facts are true, there are many other facts that are also true. The facts are that Sanders has way more independent supporters, many of which that could not vote in the closed primaries.

The second fact is that the Democrats must understand how horrible Hillary Clinton is for the Democratic nominee. She has had many years in public service, and after all this time, many Americans do not trust her, nor believe she is an ethical person. For whatever grievance citizens have with Clinton, Sanders supporters will not *get in line* and vote for Clinton because of course she is a better choice than Donald Trump. This will be the first general election I plan to participate in, and I do not plan to tarnish my voting record by voting for someone I do not politically agree with. Not to mention being told to vote for someone just because they are better than Trump is not setting the bar very high for President.

Our current primaries are a terrible indication of how our populace will vote in the general because as shown above, less than **25%** of the electorate voted. If the democrats are smart, they make Sanders their nominee. If not, then I hope either he joins a third party, or make his own party. If not, then I will write in his name and urge others to do the same. No longer shall we allow establishment politicians to dictate the destruction of our nation. Considering the general populace is larger than the establishment, it is time the establishment falls in line.

This is why the major political parties have way more power than ever intended by our constitution. While I believe they should choose a process that determines their party's nominee for president, the Republicans and Democrats should not be controlling who the main two candidates for president are year after year. Every election we keep getting candidates that the populace never wants. This election is by far the worst case scenario in which the major political party's presumptive nominees both have the highest unfavorable ratings in US history.

Now before discussing a system to change this corruption, the following is an excerpt from our first president, George Washington's farewell address that truly sums up the problems that we face currently.

> *I have already intimated to you the danger of Parties in the State, with particular reference to the founding of them on Geographical discriminations. Let me now take a more comprehensive view, & warn you in the most solemn manner against the baneful effects of the Spirit of Party, generally.*

> *This Spirit, unfortunately, is inseperable from our nature, having its root in the strongest passions of the human Mind. It exists under different shapes in all Governments, more or less stifled, controuled, or repressed; but in those of the popular form it is seen in its greatest rankness and is truly their worst enemy.*

> *The alternate domination of one faction over another, sharpened by the spirit of revenge natural to party dissention, which in different ages & countries has perpetrated the most horrid enormities, is itself a frightful*

despotism. But this leads at length to a more formal and permanent despotism. The disorders & miseries, which result, gradually incline the minds of men to seek security & repose in the absolute power of an Individual: and sooner or later the chief of some prevailing faction more able or more fortunate than his competitors, turns this disposition to the purposes of his own elevation, on the ruins of Public Liberty.

Without looking forward to an extremity of this kind (which nevertheless ought not to be entirely out of sight) the common & continual mischiefs of the spirit of Party are sufficient to make it the interest and the duty of a wise People to discourage and restrain it.

It serves always to distract the Public Councils and enfeeble the Public Administration. It agitates the Community with ill founded Jealousies and false alarms, kindles the animosity of one part against another, foments occasionally riot & insurrection. It opens the door to foreign influence & corruption, which find a facilitated access to the government itself through the channels of party passions. Thus the policy and the will of one country, are subjected to the policy and will of another.

There is an opinion that parties in free countries are useful checks upon the Administration of the Government and serve to keep alive the spirit of Liberty. This within certain limits is probably true--and in Governments of a Monarchical cast Patriotism may look with endulgence, if not with favour, upon the spirit of party. But in those of the popular character, in Governments purely elective, it is a spirit not to be encouraged. From their natural tendency, it is certain there will always be enough of that spirit for every salutary purpose. And there being constant danger of excess, the effort ought to be, by force of public opinion, to mitigate & assuage it. A fire not to be quenched; it demands a uniform vigilance to prevent its bursting into a flame, lest instead of warming it should consume...”

It is a shame these words fell on deaf ears. Our history has been overtaken by a struggle between two political parties and allowing our nation to fall apart. Our politicians have been so concerned to keep power, that they forget the way to be re-elected is to do your damn job and pass legislation to improve the nation and the lives of its citizens.

We must have politicians that can discuss middle ground. Not to say that people should compromise on their beliefs, but rather understand there are more than two thoughts on any subject. Through listening to all sides of a situation can a better solution be proposed. It is why my proposal calls for more political parties to have an equal chance in winning federal election positions. The reason for this being our nation has grown and changed over the years, and thus there are more ideas then what can be represented by two political parties. Every citizen of any nation is neither going to fall in category A or B every time on every situation.

This is the reason why gridlock exists in our Congress. The American public's interest has been removed from every issue, and replaced by an ideological battle between Republicans and Democrats. Between this and corporations paying each side of the aisle to do their bidding, is why our nation is falling apart. It is why the American middle class is disappearing, and why America has been unable to lead in world affairs.

Our nation is distracted by issues that should have been answered years ago. Health insurance for example is a problem that could have been solved had we took the advice of some of our closest allies. Looking at a majority of nations with single-payer systems, they are operational and provide affordable healthcare to all citizens. To do this though we need a tax system that can afford the expenditures. To do that though we need a congress and overall government that represents the people, and not the current oligarchy of corporate elites, corporate media elites, and the political establishments of both the Republican and Democratic parties.

So how could a new federal election system operate to provide a better democracy to America? After all, this will not be the first time an amendment after the *Bill of Rights* could change how the election process functions, or who is allowed to vote in those elections. These include the: **12**[th], **15**[th], **17**[th], **19**[th], **20**[th], **22**[ed], **23**[rd], **24**[th], and the **26**[th] amendments. As you can see over **50%** of the amendments after the first ten where on fixing the election process and increasing democracy to everyone.

The problem is that the last amendment, the **27**[th] was ratified **May 7**[th] **1992**. It has been **24** years since we updated our constitution, a document designed for solutions to be implemented when problems to the wellbeing of our nation appear. Much has changed in **24** years, and that is why the framework I have discussed thus far spells out the specifics of what will become the parts of the next constitutional amendment.

The next objective to bring democracy back to America is limiting the power currently held by the Republican and Democratic parties. We need politicians to argue over policy again, and accomplish tasks. I am not advocating removing those in the establishment from power, but rather allowing more parties to compete fairly in federal elections. If those who are currently in power not voting in a way that represents their constituency, then there should be several candidates with alternative viewpoints ready to fight for that seat in Congress. Their status as a senator, or representative is a privilege, not a right. If they wish to continue their job, then they need to represent everyone in their state and country, not just their donors.

There will be a disclaimer stating that only two representatives from the same party may run in the primary. This way we will never again see the "united" Republican party's **17** visions of our nation's future. To summarize the Republican primary this year, there are no better words to use than those used by John Oliver on his show *Last Week Tonight*. During his show on **March 6th 2016**, to discuss the election after *Super Tuesday*, it was called the: *Clowntown Fuck-The-World Shitshow 2016.*

This is a name I could not agree more with, as the Republican party has been an embarrassment. Between the constant discussions of trying to bomb the middle east more than the other, the constant racist and xenophobic remarks, and everything Trump said, why are Republicans and the mainstream media wondering how Trump ended up the nominee? A majority of the Republican base voting for Trump are probably just as racist and bigoted as him.

For the rest of Trump supporters, they are just disenfranchised voters that are tired of establishment politics. The phenomenon of Trump's rise is eerily similar to the vision as described in George Washington's farewell address. As stated when spirit of party goes unchecked, "*The disorders & miseries, which result, gradually incline the minds of men to seek security & repose in the absolute power of an Individual: and sooner or later the chief of some prevailing faction more able or more fortunate than his competitors, turns this disposition to the purposes of his own elevation, on the ruins of Public Liberty.*"

Due to the inactions of establishment politics, many people look to Trump as a stronger alternative to change the failing system. Just as fascists do, the prey on the fears of the people, and find scapegoats to blame the problems on, in order to increase credibility. In defense of the Republican party, Trump is not the majority favorite amongst Republicans. The Party hurt itself from there being so many voices trying to represent this very split party.

As in the Democratic party, the Republicans also had several candidates that are not true Republicans as Senator Sander's is not a real Democrat. However, these candidates needed to run as a major party candidate just for their messages to be heard, and be given a fighting chance to succeed in the election.

To increase democracy, it is time to have a primary that is open to all voters, and allows all candidates of all parties to debate against each other. The truth is there are other political parties in the US. The problem is the Democrats and Republicans have worked there hardest to make sure they never became actual candidates in any federal election. So once this is changed, what could a new system look like?

Currently the FEC requires presidential candidates to register once their campaigns receive or spend more than **$5,000**. That part can be the same, but the difference will be instead of allowing parties to conduct their own primaries and then have a general election; the primary and general election will be done under the direction of the FEC. No more should wealthy and political establishments pick two corporatist candidates and force us to now choose the lesser of two evils.

Those who announce their candidacy from any party will run in the same primary. Considering how the previous primary was over a year long, the election process should all be done in the same year as the actual general election. So assuming this gets enacted for the election in **2020**, imagine a system that in January to February, candidates will announce their candidacy.

As to how parties determine their nominees, that should still remain up to them. The important thing is they will no longer control the final outcomes of candidates in the election process run by the FEC. That power needs to be returned to the people. One way this is accomplished is by instituting a *Top-Two* primary. What this means is once the candidates are chosen, from February to July maybe, this is when all debates and campaigning from all the candidates shall occur. Everyone will vote for the candidate of their choice once the primary is completed. The two with the highest popular votes will move on to the general election.

To ensure a fair field, it would probably be best to word it along the lines of allowing no more than ten candidates with no more than two from the same party. After all, in addition to the Republicans and Democrats, the US does have other parties like the Libertarian and Green parties. It would be such a refresher to hear a debate staged with a balance of views and opinions. That has been the most embarrassing part of watching any republican debate this election season.

The answer to every other question during these debates usually ended up involving bombing the middle east and seeing if we can make the sand glow in the dark. This is why we need debates with multiple party views. The answer to any problem is often a combination of solutions from many viewpoints. This is the only way to get the construct the best solutions, but currently our system demonizes those who try to reach agreements by reaching across the aisle.

The only way we can fix this is by allowing a government that has more politicians from every party and every part of American life. So once we have the debates, now all Americans can take some time out of their lives every four years to learn about primary candidates, and no longer have to feel obligated to be part of a political party. People can vote for the person they feel have similar political ideologies, and will truly represent them.

No longer will supporters of certain candidates feel their support was wasted in the primary process when they drop out. Nor will voters feel discouraged if they never had an opportunity to vote for their candidate before they drop out. This way the primary can now actually be an election in which the people will vet the best two people for the job. Then those two will pick their running mates and run in a general election just as it is done now.

While solving issues and reducing antiquated complications, there is one other important fact to note in both election processes. Once and for all we shall get rid of the electoral college. We already count the popular vote; it only makes sense that count actually decides the elections. It is time that America in the **21**st century is a nation of true democracy.

Citizenship vs. Legal Resident

In several areas throughout this proposal, I had talked about a new card system. By introduction of new social security cards for citizens, and new green cards for immigrants, this amendment will further explain citizenship in our nation. Our constitution originally defined US citizens as those who are natural born, or those who have become naturalized. The vagueness from the phrase *natural born* has allowed for pointless debates to take place regarding one's citizenship.

The most recent example includes Senator Ted Cruz, the Republican presidential candidate for **2016**. Despite his mother being a US citizen, she gave birth to Ted in Canada. This fact has allowed some politicians to try and make an issue of this situation stating that since he was born in Canada, he is not an American. The reason for this is because the US is one of the few remaining countries that if born on US soil, then you are given American citizenship rights.

This system is called *Jus Soli,* which comes from the Latin meaning, *right of the soil.* Many nations today now only use a system of *Jus Sanguinis, right of blood.* The latter of which makes far more sense in today's society. With increase in globalization, more people are traveling whether it be for business or pleasure. With this change in culture, Jus Soli has become antiquated.

The reason many argue that your birth certificate is what defines citizenship status is because the belief is supported by the *Fourteenth Amendment*, which states:

Section 1.

> All persons born or naturalized in the United States, and subject to the jurisdiction thereof, are citizens of the United States and of the State wherein they reside. No State shall make or enforce any law which shall abridge the privileges or immunities of citizens of the United States; nor shall any State deprive any person of life, liberty, or property, without due process of law; nor deny to any person within its jurisdiction the equal protection of the laws.

It has been the carelessness in this wording that has allowed problems to exist to this day. By allowing this to be law, a child born on US soil of parents who are not citizens, is still a US citizen. In order to be a US citizen, it only makes sense that the person's mother is a US citizen, or the person becomes naturalized through the process currently in place.

With all the reasons for an American being born overseas, or for a foreigner to be born in the United States, citizenship at birth must be reworded to be associated with birth from a mother who is a US citizen. The reason for only the mother is because the father is not always known in every pregnancy. Also in this regard, if a foreign man were to have a child with a US woman, the child would have the same citizenship of the mother. In the reversal, if a US man were to have child with a woman in a foreign nation, the child should have the same citizenship as the mother. Then if the mother is traveling, it will not matter where her child is born, if she is a US citizen, then her child will be too.

To make this work, the US is going to need another form of citizenship other than a birth certificate. The answer lies within everyone's social security card. When the program began back in **1936**, the post office was used to distribute social security cards to all citizens. These cards have since then been utilized as a personal tax ID number in addition to an account number associated with retirement benefits. Despite this card being so important in our daily lives, it does not also function as proof of citizenship.

With this amendment that will end, allowing the *Department of Homeland Security* (DHS), the IRS, and the DHHS to have one synchronized database of all current US citizens, and legal US Residents. By reissuing new Social Security cards, these cards can now be used as proof of citizenship in order to vote, provide a tax ID number for employers, determine copay amounts for healthcare, and serve as a financial account for those on disability and social security. This can be done by allocating additional resources to every US post office to create these cards at their offices.

Once these cards are designed with efficient software, and a secured server to protect the information, we can begin switching over to these cards. Anyone with a current social security card, or any other current form or document of US citizenship, can go to their local post office and obtain a new social security card. Once received, every benefit described in this book can now be accomplished by this card.

As stated all healthcare claims will go through these cards. Your copay will be dependent on the bracket your treatment falls under. Potentially, either the system could work that you pay the difference at the healthcare provider, or alternatively the DHHS pays the healthcare providers the covered portion, and then the remaining copay amount could be paid overtime through an account online. With this card also being planned to be used as a credit card, this would be another realistic function of these cards.

This card can be used to verify voting at all federal elections by utilizing the chip again. Voting machines could be created to use these chips. Once the citizens vote, the function in the chip card that allows this could then shut down temporarily to prevent citizens voting multiple times. This way in both the primary and general election, every American will have one vote again.

As in the current system, your employer will still use your social to report income to the IRS. The difference now being that as an employee, you will no longer have to fill out a W-2. Instead, based on how much your income is, your employer will correctly withhold the correct percentage based off the new income taxes. At the end of each fiscal year, the IRS can verify a person's total income against each individual source of that income.

The last benefit is the change in how those receiving disability or social security benefits would get their funds. Instead of the current costly system of printing and mailing checks, the benefits could be applied directly onto the card as direct deposit. Going back to the website earlier, the card could have an online account associated. This way just like a bank account, those receiving benefits could go online and view their card's account balance.

The final discussion is on how to fix our current immigration dilemma. It is commonly estimated that there are **11** million people living in the shadows of this nation. This includes the millions of residents from South America and millions more who came to this nation through one of the various visa programs. There is no reason that any individual who wants to be in this nation and live by its laws should be denied. I am not suggesting they become naturalized immediately. However, we need to allow them to come out of the shadows and start being taxpayers and protected by our laws and health insurance.

At **11** million people, that means there is potentially **$85.8** billion in potential income taxes if they were all working the minimum wage. This is also the reason why the single-payer system includes immigrants. For all those who are living here and contributing in our economy, then those taxes collected help fund the portion of their health insurance. With so many in the shadows afraid of deportation, it is time to offer them a solution.

The alternative solution recommended by many Republicans is often rounding them up and deporting them. This is not how those who are looking for a better life should be treated. We are a nation of laws. For those that want to be part of our nation, there is a system in place that they must be followed in order to become naturalized citizens. Until then, they should be allowed to live in this country and be part of our society.

I am not saying open up the borders, but we do need a better system that is more efficient and secure in allowing people to immigrate into the United States. The current system involves several programs each with their own set number of visas that are allowed to be applied for each year. The problem occurs when those on these visas overstay, in addition to those crossing the border illegally.

For those already here, every immigrant whether documented or undocumented will have to reapply for their immigration status. Once immigrants are legally registered, they shall receive a new green card with a similar chip. These new green cards can then be used as the immigrant's tax ID number, and to be used for health insurance purposes. It is true they broke the law by entering this nation without going through the proper procedures. However, letting them live as undocumented workers, or trying to deport them all back to their countries is unrealistic. So for all those with no criminal records, you may apply for legal status. It is important to note that this is not amnesty as I am not recommending they become naturalized citizens. They will still have to go through that process on their own, but now they can apply for a job and pay taxes.

Therefore, what could a new system look like moving forward? For every foreign visitor currently living in the US, in order to maintain their legal resident status, there should be a flat tax of **$100** per month. This tax would replace all fees during initial immigration procedures. This way anyone who is approved to immigrate to the US who does not have the monetary resources yet, can opt to have their wages garnished to pay this tax. Anyone who is visiting the nation for only several months would pay a prorated amount. For those on vacation for under a month, they will still apply for temporary green cards, but they will not pay any tax.

The state department can still determine how many people can apply for each type of visa. The change is now that every immigrant and tourist will be entered into one program, and all receive cards to be used for health insurance and tax IDs. If any immigrant then does not renew their specific visas in an appropriate amount of time, or refuse to pay the flat tax, then they should be deported. If any immigrant commits a crime, then in addition to serving the proper punishment for the crime, they shall be deported and never be allowed back in the US.

If anyone fails to register within the deadline, or tries to enter the country illegally afterwards, the punishment needs to be sufficient enough to deter further illegal immigration. While this may still be difficult, building a wall will never fix the problem. For any of the following reasons that an immigrant should be deported, a warrant shall be released for their arrest and deportation if they do not leave in a proper manner first. Once this warrant is created, the DHS can deactivate that immigrant's green card.

One area of cooperation that will benefit would come from employers. As things stand currently, if you want to work in the US, you either have a social security number as a citizen, or proper documentation as an immigrant. The new system would basically require the same credentials, social security number for citizens, and now the new program would utilize the green card number associated with each immigrant. It is imperative immigrants do not have opportunities here, without going through the immigration process legally. Once that environment is created, they will have no choice but to either immigrate legally, or not at all.

Therefore, for any employer that hires any employees under the table, and does not report their wages to the IRS shall face appropriate penalties. For the companies that are hiring illegal immigrants, this should be an additional felony requiring additional fines and prison time. Until the system discourages the use of underpaid, and undocumented workers, companies will continue to use this source of cheap labor.

Everything listed to this point can be done if we as a citizenry can stand up to the oligarchy and demand a government that works for all of us. Every problem listed throughout this book are not new problems. A majority of these issues have been ignored for decades. Just like our infrastructure, without action to repair the problems, it is only a matter of time before the system collapses. The next section is just a recap of the budget changes, and how the new income framework can afford the new welfare frameworks in addition to all current federal costs.

The New United States Budget

With all of these changes, it is now time to recap. The upper half shows the budget spent in **2015**, and how much income was taken in that year. Underneath is the financial summary of every new proposal discussed.

Current Budeget Structure 2015					
Spending Category	Amount	Percentage	*Revenue Source*		
Pensions	953.6 Billion	25.9%	Individual Income Tax	1.540	Trillion
Health Care	1.028 Trillion	27.9%	Corporate Income Tax	343.8	Billion
Education	133.8 Billion	3.6%	Social Insurance Taxes	1.065	Trillion
Defense	797.9 Billion	21.6%	Excise Taxes	43.2	Billion
Welfare	361.9 Billion	9.8%	Other	256.9	Billion
Protection	34.0 Billion	0.9%	Total Revenue	3.249	Trillion
Transportation	89.5 Billion	2.4%	Federal Defecit	438.4	Billion
General Governemnt	43.7 Billion	1.2%	Total US Debt	18.120	Trillion
Other Spending	22.4 Billion	0.6%			
Interest	223.2 Billion	6.1%			
Total Spending	3.688 Trillion				

Proposed Budeget Structure 2017					
Spending Category	Amount	Percentage			
Department of Health and Human Services	4.235 Trillion	75.6%	Single-Payer Insurance System	2.832 Trillion	
			Social Security & Disability	1.403 Trillion	
Department of Education	133.8 Billion	2.4%	Total Estimated DHHS Budget	4.235 Trillion	
Department of Defense	797.9 Billion	14.2%			
Department of Transportation	89.5 Billion	1.6%			
Department of Labor	56.0 Billion	1.0%			
General Governemnt	43.7 Billion	0.8%			
Other Spending	22.4 Billion	0.4%			
Interest	223.2 Billion	4.0%			
Total Spending	5.602 Trillion				
Revenue Source					
Proposed Income Tax	2.227 Trillion		Estimated Income Tax Collected	1.476 Trillion	
Proposed Excise Taxes	3.429 Trillion		Shortage from *Actual* Estimate	600.0 Billion	
Other	256.9 Billion		Unemployed Estimate	64.7 Billion	
Total Revenue	5.913 Trillion		Undocumented Workers Estimate	85.8 Billion	
Federal Surplus	311.0 Billion		Total Estimated Income Tax	2.227 Trillion	
Total US Debt	19.0 Trillion				

Every budget proposal put forth has usually been denied for one of several reasons. The one put forth in this book balances the budget. In fact, it does better than that with a **$311** billion surplus. In the new budget, all welfare programs and the budget for pensions are replaced by the single budget for the DHHS. As shown, this department will now oversee only three programs to restart. This being the single-payer health insurance program, social security and disability programs.

The only other change was adding the DOL giving them a **$56** billion to set up AmWorks. Otherwise, everything else listed in **2015**, I rewrote in the proposal with no change in the amount for them to operate. The budget for the *Department* *of Defence*, has the second highest amount allocated requesting a little under **$800** billion. While I believe this to still be way too much, it will be less challenging to get the amendment passed by not altering everything in the budget.

As a citizen of the United States, the only way I see this nation surviving the next several decades is by creating a new financial framework. We need one that is going to work for all Americans, and it is basically unanimous in agreement for change to occur to our current tax system. With this amendment, we simplify the tax code, increase wages, create a single-payer health insurance program, increase benefits for those on Social Security and Disability, and can finally begin paying off the national debt.

This framework promotes the economic growth this country needs. Once more jobs are available, the government earns more through income tax revenue. With more tax revenue, we can invest more in our education systems and infrastructure. It is a shame to think the interest payment on the national debt alone, is more than the spending on education at the federal level.

In addition, this system only works with a redesigned excise tax system like the framework discussed earlier. While this currently calculates to a surplus of **$311** billion, that is also taking into account if we get every undocumented worker, and those who are currently unemployed working at minimum wage. The *Shortage from Actual Estimate*, refers to the difference when I estimated the **2013** income tax to the actual amount collected. Since I only multiplied all taxpayers by the minimum amount in each bracket, the result was my estimate was approximately **$600** billion less.

Therefore, the total budget could be enough to cover the costs. With as many variables in play, it is difficult to say that enough money is raised across the budget. Once an amendment like this is passed, and the programs are written, the next job in Congress needs to be paying off the national debt. Once this happens, or if this framework brings in more income then calculated, we can invest more in our education and infrastructure. The current plan accounts for the excise tax on stock trades set at **5%** with approximately **$63** trillion in stocks traded annually. This accounts for the majority of the tax revenue for the entire government, which is why this particular excise tax is nonnegotiable.

While I am sure investors may fight this tooth and nail, this is the next logical step forward. The tradeoff is there is no longer taxes on the capital gains of stocks. Therefore, even hedge funds will no longer have to pay taxes on their capital gains. The joy is now, instead of those companies and CEO's hiding their money in Zurich or the Cayman Islands, now all taxes must be paid during the transaction of when stocks are traded.

During the financial crisis we bailed out Wall Street. It is now time for the government to get that money back, and more importantly begin providing for the welfare of all Americans again. Thus, for arguments sake if the stock markets annual value is still only **$63** trillion, then an additional **1%** in taxes would equate to **$630** billion in additional revenue. Therefore, until we can get everyone employed, and pay off some of this national debt, I would ask the excise tax on stocks to begin at **7%**. This way an additional **$1.260** trillion will be collected to guarantee enough revenue to pay for all welfare programs, and we can begin paying off the national debt and reduce the interest payment.

At seven cents on the dollar per stock trade, we can move our nation in the proper direction again. All while providing minimal financial strain on investors and our wealthy. As this was the nation that allowed them to become wealthy, it is time they begin paying their fair share. As stated there are many trade-offs that make the system balance for the universal gain for citizens, businesses, and government.

We as a nation have to be brave, and embrace change. The image at the bottom shows the proposed breakdown of the new percentage based budget with a **7%** excise tax on stock trades. The total revenue would be approximately **$7.173** trillion. This allows plenty of revenue to fund all programs, while beginning to pay off the debt.

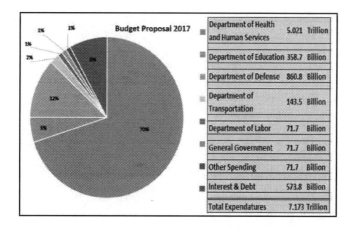

With an increase in taxes, more money is allocated to every department when based on percentages. It is for that reason, once we can balance the budget with more income being derived from the income tax, we can lower the excise taxes.

Therefore, if we want to expand programs, or invest more in any department, these percentages can always be readjusted. For reference, on the next page shows the excise tax break down with the change, raising the excise tax on stock market trades to **7%**.

Group	Products to be Taxed	Tax Rate	Estimated Income
Tobacco Products	Cigarettes, Cigarillos, Cigars, Chewing Tobacco, Loose Tobacco, E-Cigs and Vapor Accessories, Rolling Papers & Blunt Raps	25%	$25,773,000,000
Marijuana Products	Recreational Marijuana Sold Through Dispensaries, All Marijuana Edibles, All Marijuana Smoking Devices.	25%	$3,587,138,875
Alcoholic Beverages	Beer, Wine, and Liquor Sales Sold at Retail, Bars, and Resteraunts	25%	$18,675,000,000
Firearms & Ammunition	All Firearms & Ammunition Sold at Stores (In Store & Online) & Gun Shows	25%	$775,000,000
Vehicles	Retail Prices for Vehicles Bought, Leased, Rented & All Vehicle Parts	25%	$181,527,500,000
Fossil Fuels	Sale of all Fossil Fuels (Coal, Oil, Gasoline and Natural Gas)	25%	$48,617,250,000
Stock Market	Percent Tax on Purchase & Sale of US Stocks	7%	$4,410,000,000,000
		Total	$4,688,954,889,000

Constitutional Amendment XXVIII

The final part is now writing an amendment to enact everything. As mentioned, it has been **24** years since a new amendment, and with the numerous problems facing our nation, we cannot hold off any longer. The common question asked is how an amendment is passed. This is answered in *Article V* of the US constitution:

The Congress, whenever two thirds of both Houses shall deem it necessary, shall propose Amendments to this Constitution, or, on the Application of the Legislatures of two thirds of the several States, shall call a Convention for proposing Amendments, which, in either Case, shall be valid to all Intents and Purposes, as Part of this Constitution, when ratified by the Legislatures of three fourths of the several States, or by Conventions in three fourths thereof, as the one or the other Mode of Ratification may be proposed by the Congress; Provided that no Amendment which may be made prior to the Year One thousand eight hundred and eight shall in any Manner affect the first and fourth Clauses in the Ninth Section of the first Article; and that no State, without its Consent, shall be deprived of its equal Suffrage in the Senate.

To the current date, all **17** amendments after the *Bill of Rights* have only been ratified after being proposed through Congress. Since a majority of our Congress is under corporate influence, the idea of them proposing an amendment, let alone two thirds of both houses approving it seems unlikely. Therefore, in addition to the historical need for a new amendment, the only other way to acquire this is through a constitutional convention called forth by the states.

While this has not yet happened in our history, now may be the time for the States to call a convention. With **50** states currently in our union, only **34** are needed to meet the two thirds requirement. Regardless of the method of initiation, an amendment does not become ratified until approved by three-fourths of the states.

Going through the proposal, we have discussed many policies. The budget is balanced while increasing benefits, and economic growth. Despite the many changes, the system will be simplified to balance the budget while providing unprecedented economic growth. In order to bring this vision into reality, the next amendment to the US constitution shall resemble the following.

Amendment XXVIII

Section 1.

The United States Congress shall pass a percentage based budget each year in order to guarantee more money is not being spent then taken in. This budget is to allocate enough funds to function all major government departments, programs, and pay off federal debts. Each year the Congress shall review all expenditures by each department and program to determine wasteful spending, and prepare the next year's budget.

Section 2.

Once ratified by three-fourths of state legislatures, the minimum wage shall be set to **$15.00** an hour. Thus the *Full Time Equivalent* value is to equal the minimum wage multiplied by forty hours for fifty-two weeks. Therefore, at **$15.00** an hour the FTE is **$31,200** a year. This can only be raised by two-thirds approval of both houses of Congress.

This minimum wage is to be applied to all positons in every industry. Regardless of tips or any other compensation, employers at minimum must pay workers **$15.00** for every hour officially clocked in.

Section 3.

The *Income Tax* will collect revenue derived from incomes from employment, income on interest, and income from dividends. Capital gains will no longer be included as income taxable under the income tax. There will be five brackets including: **(1)** those making less than the *Full Time Equivalent* at **20%**, **(2)** those making the *Full Time Equivalent* to under **$100,000** at **25%**, **(3)** **$100,000** to under **$500,000** at **30%**, **(4)** **$500,000** to under **$1,000,000** at **35%**, **(5)** those making over **$1,000,000** to be taxed at **50%**. Changes to the tax brackets may only occur with two-thirds approval of both houses of Congress.

All employers may only hire workers in the US that have a valid social security number, or legal residents with a valid green card number. Any employers who are not reporting wages to the IRS, or paying employees less than **$15.00** an hour shall face penalties including fines, and imprisonment.

Section 4.

All excise taxes shall be a percentage on the consumer retail price which shall remain uniform across all products listed in the taxed category. Consumers are to include all businesses and individuals. All current excise taxes are to be replaced by the following groups of products.

Group	Products to be Taxed	Tax Rate
Tobacco Products	Cigarettes, Cigarillos, Cigars, Chewing Tobacco, Loose Tobacco, E-Cigs and Vapor Accessories, Rolling Papers & Blunt Raps	25%
Marijuana Products	Recreational Marijuana Sold Through Dispensaries, All Marijuana Edibles, All Marijuana Smoking Devices.	25%
Alcoholic Beverages	Beer, Wine, and Liquor Sales Sold at Retail, Bars, and Resteraunts	25%
Firearms & Ammunition	All Firearms & Ammunition Sold at Stores (In Store & Online) & Gun Shows	25%
Vehicles	Retail Prices for Vehicles Bought, Leased, Rented & All Vehicle Parts	25%
Fossil Fuels	Sale of all Fossil Fuels (Coal, Oil, Gasoline and Natural Gas)	25%
Stock Market	Percent Tax on Purchase & Sale of US Stocks	7%

Changes to product groups or tax rates may only occur with two-thirds approval of both houses of Congress. The states and territories will have final say in laws and regulations regarding what products are allowed in their jurisdiction. The states, territories, and local governments may also raise taxes on the same excised products and services as they see fit.

Section 5.

The *Department of Health and Human Services* will be required to oversee the programs of a single-payer health insurance program, Social Security, and Disability. The benefits distributed for those on Social Security and Disability shall be equal to the set minimum wage *Full Time Equivalent* value. The DHHS will provide a price guide to work with medical providers to provide fair reimbursement for medical services. In addition, they will work with the DEA to determine which medications will be on the government formulary. The states and territories will retain final say as to which products are, or are not allowed for distribution in their jurisdiction. The framework for the single-payer system to be used by the DHHS:

Group	Medically Necessary	Copay
Children < 3	100%	0%
Children 3 – 17	90%	10%
Adults 18 – 69*	85%	15%
Adults 70* +	100%	0%
US Veterans	100%	0%
Legal Residents & Tourists	80%	20%

	Medical Care	Dental	Vision	Pharmaceuticals
Medical Care Asscoiated with Attacks	100%			
Cancer & Emergency Outbreaks	100%			
All Birth Related Healthcare	100%			
Medically Necessary	Max %			
Coverage For Accidents	75%			
Cosmetic	0%			

Section 6.

The budget allocated to the *Department of Labor* shall be used to create offices and websites with the main purpose of providing a free service for employers to find employees, and employees to find employers.

Section 7.

All federal elections will be run under FEC guidelines. Federal elections shall be operated in two parts. The primary will take place from **February 1st** of election year to **July 3rd** of the same year. Those who wish to run for office must announce their candidacy and meet FEC guidelines beginning **January 1st** of election year to **January 31st**. No more than ten candidates may run with no more than two from any one political party in any federal election for a single position. Debates are to be funded by the FEC during the primary process until election day on **July 4th**.

All citizens in states and territories will vote on **July 4th** from **9 AM** to **9 PM** local times. Once all votes are counted, those in first and second place in total popular vote shall move onto the general election. Those running for the presidency shall announce running mates for Vice President soon after. During the general election the FEC will once again fund debates until election day in November.

Section 8.

All Districts and Territories shall each have representation in both houses of Congress. For the House of Representatives, each shall elect the same number of representatives equal to the number of representatives for the smallest State. For the Senate, each District and Territory shall elect one Senator.

Section 9.

The rights of all US citizens to vote in any federal election shall not be infringed as long as they provide proof of their citizenship by use of their social security card. The *Department of Health and Human Services* shall design and maintain a social security chip card to replace the current paper social security I.D. numbers. Once all programs are designed and ready for the new program, they shall be distributed for free as a local service of all *US Post Offices*. All current US citizens must bring a current social security card, or any other current ID that proves citizenship to receive a new card.

All cards will contain information for citizenship including: name, date of birth, social security number, photo, and chip for financial transactions. These cards must be renewed every ten years. If a card is lost or stolen, the citizen is responsible for providing proof of identity, and paying the cost for a new card. In addition to proof of citizenship for federal elections, these cards will be used by citizens to apply for passports and state licenses. The IRS shall also receive a synced copy of current social security numbers to match with employer payroll records. Any employer who hires an employee with an invalid social security number will be notified.

The chip on the card shall be used for three purposes.

(1) The *Department of Health and Human Services* will keep record of all social security accounts. Health providers will be able to accept these cards in order to charge the bill to the *Department of Health and Human Services*. Depending on your age and reasoning for treatments, the copay amount will be determined.

(2) For citizens that qualify for Social Security or Disability, their benefits shall be equal to the *Full Time Equivalent* determined by the minimum wage. The bi-weekly payment shall be directly deposited onto their social security card. These cards can then be used like a normal debit or credit card.

(3) The *Federal Election Commission* will also have this database for reference on elections days. The cards will be used for proof of citizenship to vote, and then once voted your social security card would be flagged as voted so you cannot vote again until after the polls close.

Section 10.

All donations given to political campaigns may only come from US citizens. All donations to campaigns must be given with the donators social security number. The FEC will enforce campaign finance laws by reviewing all donations to ensure no more than **$2,000** per person is donated to candidates running for seats in the House of Representatives, no more than **$3,000** per person is donated to candidates running for seats in the Senate, and no more than **$5,000** per person for those running for President. This can only be raised by two-thirds approval of both houses of Congress.

Section 11.

A new immigration program will be created and run by the *Department of Homeland Security* for US immigrants. All current immigrants in this nation must register with the department to become a legal resident, and receive the benefits that entails. Once created, new green cards shall be given to registered immigrants which will also contain a chip to be used for healthcare. For this reason, the *Department of Health and Human Services* will have a synced database with that of the *Department of Homeland Security*. The IRS shall also have a copy to match with employer payroll records. These cards must be renewed every one year.

Those who wish to live in this nation as immigrants until they can become citizens through the naturalization process must register. Legal residents will be required to pay a **$100** flat tax per month stayed in the US. No tax will be issued for those in the US under a month. Once registered, the new green card will allow you to receive healthcare, and become employed in the US if desired.

Those who fail to pay the monthly flat tax, or fail to renew their green cards shall be notified. Any legal resident who commits a crime, or after a certain passage of time fail to pay the tax or renew their card, a warrant shall be placed out for their arrest to be deported after serving any time sentenced for conviction of a crime.

Section 12.

The Congress shall have the power to enforce by appropriate legislation, the provisions of this article.

References

2015 Aetna Annual Report, Financial Report to Shareholders. Rep. N.p.: n.p., n.d. Apr. 2016. Web. 1 July 2016. <http://www.aetna.com/investors-aetna/assets/documents/2016-annual-meeting/2015-aetna-annual-report-financial-report.pdf>.

"Buckley v. Valeo." *Wikipedia.* Wikimedia Foundation, 8 June 2016. Web. 02 July 2016. <https://en.wikipedia.org/wiki/Buckley_v._Valeo>.

Chantrill, Christopher. "Government Revenue Details." *: Federal State Local for 2013.* N.p., n.d. Web. 01 July 2016. <http://www.usgovernmentrevenue.com/year_revenue_2013USbn_17bs1n#usgs302>.

Chantrill, Christopher. "US Federal Budget Analyst." *US Federal Budget Actual Spending Breakdown 2010-2015.* N.p., n.d. Web. 01 July 2016. <http://www.usfederalbudget.us/federal_budget_actual>.

"Colorado Marijuana Tax Data." *Home.* Colorado Department of Revenue, 2016. Web. 01 July 2016. <https://www.colorado.gov/pacific/revenue/colorado-marijuana-tax-data>.

"Company Facts." *Company Facts.* Walmart, n.d. Web. 02 July 2016. <http://corporate.walmart.com/newsroom/company-facts>.

Confessore, Nicholas, and Karen Yourish. "$2 Billion Worth of Free Media for Donald Trump." *The New York Times.* The New York Times, 15 Mar. 2016. Web. 02 July 2016. <http://www.nytimes.com/2016/03/16/upshot/measuring-donald-trumps-mammoth-advantage-in-free-media.html>.

"Economic Facts About U.S. Tobacco Production and Use." *Centers for Disease Control and Prevention*. Centers for Disease Control and Prevention, 08 Apr. 2016. Web. 01 July 2016. <http://www.cdc.gov/tobacco/data_statistics/fact_sheets/economics/econ_facts/index.htm#sales>.

"Employer Costs for Employee Compensation News Release." *U.S. Bureau of Labor Statistics*. U.S. Bureau of Labor Statistics, 09 Sept. 2015. Web. 01 July 2016. <http://www.bls.gov/news.release/archives/ecec_09092015.htm>.

Fan, Katherine, Shantanu Nigam, and Sissi Yang. "Who Benefits More from Obamacare: Wal-Mart or Employees?" Web log post. *Corporation360*. N.p., 30 Jan. 2015. Web. 01 July 2016. <https://corporation360.wordpress.com/2015/01/30/who-benefits-more-from-obamacare-wal-mart-or-employees/>.

"FAQs ON AP's VOTE-COUNTING NETWORK." Associated Press, n.d. Web. 02 July 2016. <http://ap.org/products-services/elections/FAQs>.

"The FEC and the Federal Campaign Finance Law." *Federal Election Commission*. Federal Election Commission, Jan. 2015. Web. 02 July 2016. <http://www.fec.gov/pages/brochures/contrib.shtml>.

"Federal Election Campaign Act." *Wikipedia*. Wikimedia Foundation, 19 May 2016. Web. 02 July 2016. <https://en.wikipedia.org/wiki/Federal_Election_Campaign_Act>.

"Federal Excise Tax Rates, 1944-2008. Selected Years." *Http://taxfoundation.org/article/federal-excise-tax-rates-1944-2008-selected-years*. N.p., n.d. Web. 1 July 2016. <http://taxfoundation.org/article/federal-excise-tax-rates-1944-2008-selected-years>.

"First National Bank of Boston v. Bellotti." *Wikipedia*. Wikimedia Foundation, 28 May 2016. Web. 02 July 2016. <https://en.wikipedia.org/wiki/First_National_Bank_of_Boston_v._Bellotti>.

"Front-Runners Hope to Vault Ahead in Big Contests." *The Wall Street Journal* 15 Mar. 2016, Vol. CCLXVII ed., No. 61 sec.: 1. Print.

"Gas Station Statistics." *Statistic Brain*. N.p., n.d. Web. 01 July 2016. <http://www. statisticbrain.com/gas-station-statistics/>.

Gilens, Martin, and Benjamin I. Page. *Testing Theories of American Politics: Elites, Interest Groups, and Average Citizens*. Thesis. Princeton University, 2014. N.p.: n.p., n.d. American Political Science Association, Sept. 2014. Web. 2 July 2016. <https://scholar.princeton.edu/sites/default/files/mgilens/files/ gilens_and_page_2014_-testing_theories_of_american_politics.doc.pdf>.

Greenberg, Scott. "How Many Taxpayers Fall Into Each Income Tax Bracket?" *Tax Foundation*. N.p., 15 Oct. 2015. Web. 1 July 2016. <http://taxfoundation.org/ blog/how-many-taxpayers-fall-each-income-tax-bracket>.

"Health Insurance Coverage of the Total Population." *KFF.org*. Kaiser Family Foundation, n.d. Web. 01 July 2016. <http://kff.org/other/state-indicator/ total-population/>.

Hernandez, Elizabeth. "Colorado Monthly Marijuana Sales Eclipse $100 Million Mark." *The Denver Post*. N.p., 09 Oct. 2015. Web. 01 July 2016. <http://www.denverpost. com/2015/10/09/colorado-monthly-marijuana-sales-eclipse-100-million-mark/>.

"Historical." *CMS.gov Centers for Medicare & Medicaid Services*. N.p., 03 Dec. 2015. Web. 01 July 2016. <https://www.cms.gov/research-statistics- data-and-systems/statistics-trends-and-reports/nationalhealthexpenddata/ nationalhealthaccountshistorical.html>.

"History of Federal Minimum Wage Rates Under the Fair Labor Standards Act, 1938 - 2009." *United States Department of Labor Wage and Hour Division (WHD)*. United States Department of Labor, n.d. Web. 02 July 2016. <https://www.dol. gov/whd/minwage/chart.htm>.

"How Are Social Security Benefits Calculated?" *My Retirement Paycheck*. National Endowment for Financial Education, 2016. Web. 01 July 2016. <http://www. myretirementpaycheck.org/social-security/how-are-benefits-calculated.aspx>.

"The Individual Mandate Penalties." Web log post. *You Think You Know*. N.p., 13 Aug. 2013. Web. 01 July 2016. <https://justgngr.wordpress.com/2013/08/13/ the-individual-mandate-penalties/>.

Jones, Jeffrey M. "Democratic, Republican Identification Near Historical Lows." *Gallup.com*. Gallup, 11 Jan. 2016. Web. 02 July 2016. <http://www.gallup.com/poll/188096/democratic-republican-identification-near-historical-lows.aspx>.

Jones, Jeffrey M. "In U.S., 58% Back Legal Marijuana Use." *Gallup.com*. Gallup, 21 Oct. 2015. Web. 02 July 2016. <http://www.gallup.com/poll/186260/back-legal-marijuana.aspx>.

"Liquor Store Sales in the United States, 2015 | Statistic." *Statista*. N.p., n.d. Web. 01 July 2016. <http://www.statista.com/statistics/197630/annual-liquor-store-sales-in-the-us-since-1992/>.

"Market Data [U.S. Car Rental Market]." *File Viewer - Auto Rental News*. Auto Rental News, 2016. Web. 01 July 2016. <http://www.autorentalnews.com/fileviewer/2230.aspx>.

N.p., n.d. Web. <www.google.com>.

Our Amazing World. "Bernie Sanders vs Rand Paul: Healthcare & Drug Company Corruption." *YouTube*. YouTube, 22 Aug. 2015. Web. 01 July 2016. <https://www.youtube.com/watch?v=e2WIwv_4sY0>.

"PieChartSourcesExpenditures2014." (n.d.): n. pag. Centers for Medicare & Medicaid Services. Web. 1 July 2016. <https://www.cms.gov/Research-Statistics-Data-and-Systems/Statistics-Trends-and-Reports/NationalHealthExpendData/Downloads/PieChartSourcesExpenditures2014.pdf>.

Pollack, Andrew, and Matthew Goldstein. "Martin Shkreli All but Gloated Over Huge Drug Price Increases, Memos Show." *The New York Times*. The New York Times, 02 Feb. 2016. Web. 01 July 2016. <http://www.nytimes.com/2016/02/03/business/drug-makers-calculated-price-increases-with-profit-in-mind-memos-show.html?_r=1>.

Pollack, Andrew. "Drug Goes From $13.50 a Tablet to $750, Overnight." *The New York Times*. The New York Times, 20 Sept. 2015. Web. 01 July 2016. <http://www.nytimes.com/2015/09/21/business/a-huge-overnight-increase-in-a-drugs-price-raises-protests.html>.

Popken, Ben. "America's Gun Business, by the Numbers." *CNBC*. N.p., 02 Oct. 2015. Web. 01 July 2016. <http://www.cnbc.com/2015/10/02/americas-gun-business-by-the-numbers.html>.

"Population Information and Statistics From Every City, State and County in the US." *Information and Statistics From Every City, State and County in the US.* Suburban Stats, n.d. Web. 01 July 2016. <https://suburbanstats.org/>.

"Recreational Marijuana Taxes." *Recreational Marijuana Taxes.* Department of Revenue Washington State, n.d. Web. 01 July 2016. <http://dor.wa.gov/Content/AboutUs/StatisticsAndReports/stats_RMJTaxes.aspx>.

Rosenberg, Alex. "Are Valeant, Philidor and R&O All the Same Company?" *Trading Nation.* CNBC, 23 Oct. 2015. Web. 02 July 2016. <http://www.cnbc.com/2015/10/22/are-valeant-philidor-and-ro-all-the-same-company.html>.

Russell, Jason. "Look at How Many Pages Are in the Federal Tax Code." *Washington Examiner.* N.p., 29 June 2016. Web. 01 July 2016. <http://www.washingtonexaminer.com/look-at-how-many-pages-are-in-the-federal-tax-code/article/2563032>.

Snyder, Riley. "No, Bernie Sanders Didn't Retroactively Win Nevada." *Politifact Nevada.* Politifact, 7 Apr. 2016. Web. 02 July 2016. <http://www.politifact.com/nevada/statements/2016/apr/07/blog-posting/no-bernie-sanders-didnt-retroactively-win-nevada/>.

Social Security Administration. "The First Social Security Number and the Lowest Number." *Social Security Numbers.* Social Security Administration, n.d. Web. 02 July 2016. <https://www.ssa.gov/history/ssn/firstcard.html>.

"Social Security." *Beneficiary Statistics.* Social Security Administration, n.d. Web. 01 July 2016. <https://www.ssa.gov/oact/STATS/OASDIbenies.html>.

"Social Security." *Primary Insurance Amount.* Social Security Administration, n.d. Web. 01 July 2016. <https://www.ssa.gov/oact/cola/piaformula.html>.

"Social Security." *What Is the Average Monthly Benefit for a Retired Worker?* Social Security Administration, 11 Mar. 2016. Web. 01 July

2016. <https://faq.ssa.gov/link/portal/34011/34019/Article/3736/ What-is-the-average-monthly-benefit-for-a-retired-worker>.

"Social Security." *What Is the Maximum Retirement Benefit Payable?* Social Security Administration, n.d. Web. 02 July 2016. <https://faq.ssa.gov/link/portal/34011/34019/article/3735/ what-is-the-maximum-social-security-retirement-benefit-payable>.

Staff of the Joint Committee on Taxation. "Impose a Tax on Financial Transactions." *Congressional Budget Office*. N.p., 15 Nov. 2013. Web. 01 July 2016. <https:// www.cbo.gov/budget-options/2013/44855>.

Street, Chriss W. "Democratic Establishment Steals Nevada Caucus Win From Bernie Sanders." *Breitbart News*. Breitbart, 16 May 2016. Web. 02 July 2016. <http://www.breitbart.com/2016-presidential-race/2016/05/16/ democrat-establishment-robs-bernie-sanders-nevada-caucus-win/>.

"Super PACs." *Open Secrets.org Center for Responsive Politics*. The Center for Responsive Politics, 24 June 2016. Web. 02 July 2016. <https://www.opensecrets. org/pacs/superpacs.php?cycle=2016>.

"Tax Brackets." *2015-2016*. N.p., n.d. Web. 01 July 2016. <http://www.bankrate. com/finance/taxes/tax-brackets.aspx>.

"Tillman Act of 1907." *Wikipedia*. Wikimedia Foundation, 29 Feb. 2016. Web. 02 July 2016. <https://en.wikipedia.org/wiki/Tillman_Act_of_1907>.

"Topic: Bar & Nightclub Industry." *Www.statista.com*. N.p., n.d. Web. 01 July 2016. <http://www.statista.com/topics/1752/bars-and-nightclubs/>.

"Trading Day." *Wikipedia*. Wikimedia Foundation, 29 Mar. 2016. Web. 01 July 2016. <https://en.wikipedia.org/wiki/Trading_day>.

"Unemployed Persons by Marital Status, Race, Hispanic or Latino Ethnicity, Age, and Sex." *U.S. Bureau of Labor Statistics*. U.S. Bureau of Labor Statistics, 10 Feb. 2016. Web. 02 July 2016. <http://www.bls.gov/cps/cpsaat24.htm>.

United States. *The Bill of Rights & All Amendments*. N.p.: n.p., n.d. Web. 2 July 2016. <http://constitutionus.com/>.

United States. *The Constitution of the United States*. N.p.: n.p., n.d. Web. 02 July 2016. <http://constitutionus.com/>.

United States. *George Washington's Farewell Address*. By George Washington. N.p.: n.p., 1796. *ConText*. Web. 02 July 2016. <http://context.montpelier. org/document/715?gclid=CjwKEAjw86e4BRCnzuWGlpjLoUcSJACaHG55T FweBaugVFWRowsvMAefkJpL7qg09Sms9B8Zv6DTLxoCWgrw_wcB>.

United States. Securities and Exchange Commission. *Form 10-K*. N.p., n.d. Web. 1 July 2016. <http://www.unitedhealthgroup.com/~/media/UHG/PDF/2015/ UNH-Q4-2015-Form-10-K.ashx?la=en>.

"U.S. and World Population Clock Tell Us What You Think." *Population Clock*. United States Census Bureau, n.d. Web. 01 July 2016. <http://www.census.gov/ popclock/>.

"U.S. Auto Leasing, Loans & Sales Financing Revenue 2014 | Statistic." *Statista*. N.p., n.d. Web. 01 July 2016. <http://www.statista.com/statistics/295174/ revenue-auto-leasing-loans-and-sales-financing-in-the-us/>.

"U.S. Auto Parts Stores Revenue 2014 | Statistic." *Statista*. N.p., n.d. Web. 01 July 2016. <http://www.statista.com/statistics/292522/revenue-of-auto-parts-stores-in-the-us/>.

"U.S. New Car Dealers Revenue 2014 | Statistic." *Statista*. N.p., n.d. Web. 01 July 2016. <http://www.statista.com/statistics/292474/revenue-of-new-car-dealers-in-the-us/>.

Wall Street Journal. "How Many People Earn More than $1,000,000 Per Year In the United States?" Web log post. *Joshua Kennon Thoughts on Buisness, Politics & Life from a Private Investor*. N.p., 19 Mar. 2012. Web. 01 July 2016. <http://www.joshuakennon.com/how-many-people-earn-more-than-1000000-per-year-in-the-united-states/>.

Walmart. *Walmart 2014 Annual Report*. Rep. Walmart, n.d. Web. 2 July 2016. <https://cdn.corporate.walmart.com/66/e5/9ff9a87445949173fde56316a c5f/2014-annual-report.pdf>.

Woo, Andrew. "May 2016 National Apartment List Rent Report - Apartment List Rentonomics." *Apartment List Rentonomics*. N.p., 29 Apr. 2016. Web. 02 July 2016. <https://www.apartmentlist.com/rentonomics/united-states-rent-data-rentonomics/>.

Printed in the United States
By Bookmasters